MIKE'S MEMOIRS

Published in 2004 by

WOODFIELD PUBLISHING
Woodfield House, Babsham Lane, Bognor Regis
West Sussex PO21 5EL, England.

ISBN 1-903953-57-X

Front cover illustration:
The Author at No.3 School of Technical Training,
RAF Manston, Kent, 1934.

Mike's Memoirs

*An Airman's Recollections of Service in the
Royal Air Force 1934-1946*

F.W. 'MIKE' HUNT

Woodfield

Snug as a bug inside and out! The Author's 'pied-a-terre' – RAF Angle, Pembrokeshire, November 1941.

CONTENTS

Le Touquet, France 1940, 'Happy' airmen take a look at a bomb crater left by attackers at our airfield. Fortunately, this one missed. (see Chapter 14)

Croydon Airport 1939. Our less than comfortable billet on the floor of one of the aircraft hangars. Hardly the VIP Suite!

PREFACE

I feel you should know just how these memoirs came into being and just who was responsible. Since the end of the war we have held annual 615 Squadron reunions at our home airfield, Kenley, and it was at one of these gatherings in the 1970s that I met up again with an old friend from the Squadron, Vic Milner, who was then editor of our Squadron magazine. I had first met Vic when posted to the Squadron on its formation in 1937. It was to be a new auxiliary squadron and part of my duties was to instruct new recruits to the unit; Vic was one of these – whom I always looked upon 'my boys'.

In conversation during this meeting, Vic told me how difficult it was to find material for the magazine. Knowing that I had been a regular airman for many years and that I had served on Flying Boats, he suggested I should write something.

Despite my protests that I did not think I could do anything of this nature, as my standard of education left much to be desired, particularly my grasp of the English Language, he implored me to 'give it a go – just describe what it was like joining the RAF right from the start.' So I 'gave it a go', and the rest, as they say, is history.

Vic told me he liked what I sent him, and moreover that some of the magazine's readers had liked it too, so would I please send him a further episode. From then on, like Topsy, it has kept on growing. I apologise in advance for any errors and hiccups – I do hope that you will all forgive. Alas, I am no Barbara Cartland!

Mike Hunt, 2004

Frank (Mike) Hunt and his wife Ivy, still going strong after over 60 years.

1. The Beginning

It is a well known fact that Adolf Hitler was a man of great superstition who was greatly influenced by fortune tellers and soothsayers. Now had these influential people acquainted Adolf with news of an event that was to change the whole course of history, it is possible that Adolf would have stayed with his painting and decorating and the world would have been a healthier place to have lived in! I am, of course, referring to the day of 6th June 1934 – the day I joined the Royal Air Force!

Having already sat a preliminary exam, I presented myself as requested (most politely I must add) at Adastral House, Kingsway London on Wednesday 1st June, where about 24 other chaps joined me. We were given tea and cakes and eventually put on a most comfortable coach and transported to RAF West Drayton. This station was not used in those days for Air Traffic Control as it is today; there were not too many civilian aircraft around and hardly ever more than two of three airborne at the same time.

On arrival at W.D. we were met by a kindly and most helpful airman who told us that he was a Flight Sergeant (but were not all these F/S kindly and helpful?) and immediately we had visions of aeroplanes and actually flying! Why else would you need a Flight Sergeant? That was very promptly sorted out when he explained that a Flight Sergeant was a most important rank, which commanded the utmost respect and that it would benefit our service careers if we paid heed to this at all times. And this we duly did!

We were then taken along to a single-storey building known as a 'Thorne hut' and told that this is where we would be housed for the next few days. The Flight Sergeant then explained that before we entered this hut, he would like to tell us about something we would encounter on entering the building. He referred to this as 'the Iron Maiden', whom we would get to love even as our own mother. He said we would get very attached to this lady, that there would be times when we could barely tear ourselves away from her and that there would be many occasions when we would give anything to be enfolded in her embrace. 'Of course,' he said, 'you will at first find her hard and unyielding, but soon you will come to accept her and she will afford you many happy hours of comfort and peace. But...' he continued, 'at all times you must treat her with respect and care, for she has been known to tear a limb from a body as neatly as a doctor's scalpel and can remove a man's skin with the greatest of ease.'

With awe and wonderment we entered the hut, not knowing just what to expect and were introduced ... to the 'McDonald Bed', a service contraption constructed of angle iron and masses of springs (airmen for the use of) made in two parts, the lower half sliding into the upper half, which even included a headrest! Also supplied were three 'biscuits', each 30 inches square, which, when laid end-to-end, formed a mattress on which to lie. When new, these biscuits could well pass as enlarged breeze-blocks, but they softened with age (after about 10 years) before reverting to breezeblocks once again. The bed had a threefold purpose in life, as a bed, as a chair and as something to lay one's kit on for inspection. These were its official purposes; there were, of course, other uses, but before anyone gets the wrong idea, there were no WAAFs in the service in those days! I am referring to the jokers and pranksters who would remove all the springs from the bed, place a container of water under the bed and then await the unsuspecting occupant's return from an evening 'out on the tiles' – with the obvious outcome. Good fun, what?

Looking back over the years, however, I think most of what the Flight Sergeant said about 'her' was quite true – as I'm sure any of you familiar with this particular lady will agree!

The next day we were taken on a tour of the station. We attended a lecture and a film show at which the virtues, the wonderful prospects and the outstanding future that life in the RAF had to offer was revealed to us. We had been fed with fantastic food, better than many of us had ever had before; we had all been treated in a most courteous and considerable manner; we were most impressed. We were then told that in the morning we would be given a free travel warrant to go home for the weekend, to come back any time on Sunday and that this time was to allow us to make up our minds about joining the service.

We all did return from our weekend and when we were awakened by our Flight Sergeant on the Monday morning he said that as we had all returned it would be presumed that we wanted to join the service. We were invited to enjoy our breakfast in such a way that I well remember at the time a phrase that was going through my mind: "The condemned man ate a hearty breakfast..." But I kept my thoughts to myself.

We were asked to present ourselves, looking as neat and tidy as possible, outside the Admin Block for the enrolment ceremony, due to take place at 1100 hours. We were duly taken in *en masse* and each presented with 'the Kings Shilling' (which I still have to this day). And now we were ordered to 'fall in' outside in two lines facing the square.

Up to this point we had been addressed as 'gentlemen' and always asked in the most polite way to fulfil any tasks required, but now we were 'airmen' and being 'told' quite abruptly what to do! The change in attitude was quite remarkable, to say the least, and my thoughts went back to that 'condemned man' again. We no longer strolled back to our billet but were marched up and down the square a few times to get the hang of marching and I began to form an impression that I had been 'conned' and was not going to like the service at all.

Then we were told to be ready to move camp within 30 minutes and to take all our belongings with us.

Our transport arrived, no longer a luxurious coach but a Leyland lorry, into which we were all packed, many of us in our best and only suit, and I think the general feeling at the time was 'what the hell have we done and how can we get out of it?'

But it was too late. We were 'in the bag' and could only wonder what was in store for us when we arrived at RAF Uxbridge – for that was where we were heading – which was to be our 'home' for the next nine months.

2. The Girding of the Loins

'Uxbridge' was looked upon by most RAF personnel as their Mecca, but we recruits had other names for the place at this time. We certainly wanted to look the other way. Situated on the outskirts of London, it comprised an enormous parade square on two sides of which were the barrack blocks. There were four, three-storey blocks each side with a central staircase with dormitories for about thirty men in each. The eight blocks were each given the name of a First World War battle site: Mons, Ypres, Cambrai, Verdun etc, and were impressive in a way. At the lower end of the square was the cookhouse, the NAAFI and the recreation rooms; at the top of the square were the guardroom, 'admin' offices and the cinema. The whole area was enclosed by 12 foot high iron railings with two huge iron gates which were constantly manned by guards. The only thing missing was a moat! Did someone mention concentration camp?

So this was to be our 'home' for some while to come... and when we were told that we would not be allowed out of the camp until it was felt we could wear our uniform in a correct manner, looking smart and with a bearing befitting a member of the RAF, and that this could possibly take up to a couple of months or more, we all realised we had to accept the inevitable, and I for one did just that.

On my second day at the depot I was 'marched' with the others in my entry to the stores to be kitted out with our uniform – and what an experience this turned out to be. First I was handed three shirts which seemed to be made from a Hessian-type material; I later found out that they were! I also learnt what it must have felt like to wear a 'hair shirt'. Underwear came next, and what mirth this created. The vests were buttoned up to the neck and had long sleeves which reached below the elbow; the pants, of course, were of the long variety and had to be seen to be believed. My own issue were long enough, but reached up to my armpits and I am sure I could quite easily have hidden someone else inside them with me! Both vest and pants were made from a material known as 'flannelette' and came in two shades of lavender, light and dark. I had some of each. I cannot remember any one of us ever wearing these garments.

Boots were next on the agenda, and the issue of these caused no end of problems (shoes were definitely not allowed). The storeman asked our hat size and our collar size, looked at a chart on the wall and promptly handed us a pair of boots, saying "these will fit". These had to be worn and were possibly the hardest thing we had to get used to. All sorts of suggestions came from various quarters as to how these new boots could be made wearable – from standing them in a bucket of water for hours at a time to holding them over a steaming kettle, soaking them over-night in 'virgin' water (possible in those days but not a chance today) and the generous use of dubbing – but all to no avail. We were limping for a long while.

But the best was yet to come! The uniform. I was introduced to 'pantaloons', which were issued in place of trousers and were designed to be worn with 'puttees'. The name pantaloon was enough to make one want to throw up and when I saw a pair for the first time I nearly did just that; the only thing I could liken them to was what were known as 'ladies bloomers'. They reached just below the knee and were tight fitting; the puttees were wrapped around the leg from the ankle to the knee in a specific manner. These were strips of material supplied in roll form about four inches wide and were made from what appeared to be roofing felt. The idea was to start wrapping from the ankle, each wrap had to be correctly spaced up the leg and one had to finish when the sewn end of the puttee was in line with the side seam of the pantaloon. This was a most difficult thing to do and took months to master; it was to get me into trouble later on in the service, but more of that later.

I just could not imagine how anybody could devise such garments and expect any person wearing them to look smart and I said as much to our sergeant in charge, stating that whoever though this up should have his head examined. 'But,' said the sergeant, 'this was all designed with an object in mind. I would assume,' he continued, 'that you are not a very religious man and are not aware of what the scriptures tell us. They tell us that when Jesus cometh again he will be born of man and no one will knoweth whence he cometh. Now we in the RAF are far seeing and we are not taking any chances. We can't have Him dropping out on the parade ground and injuring Himself – so pantaloons are in!

This of course raised hoots of laughter and we all realised that he was pulling our leg. 'Come off it sarge, there must be a proper reason for such garb?' (There is really, the puttees are worn to stop the wearer being bitten by snakes and you can only wear puttees with pantaloons. And here I must say that whoever devised this form of dress possibly got it right, because neither I nor any in my entry were bitten by a snake during the entire time we were at Uxbridge!)

The remaining items of kit were handed out amidst much humour: tunics (in these days fastened tight at the neck) had sleeves that were either too long or too short and it soon became clear that the most important person on the camp was the resident tailor – an ex-ACH u/t fabric worker who, when he failed to pass was offered the tailor spot. The alterations this poor man was asked to undertake would have tried the patience of a real tailor and it was some six weeks or more before we all looked reasonable.

In those days there was no such thing as a forage cap, it was peaked hats only and you would not believe there were so many different ways to wear the same type of hat. I am sure we were the despair of our sergeant instructor.

And so, eventually, we 'aficionados' (there was so such 'bull' around by this time that the word comes readily to mind) were kitted out and ready to do battle!

3. Stiffening the Sinews

Now kitted out, but bearing no resemblance whatsoever to a fighting force, I wondered just what was in store for us next. I was soon to find out! I and my companions would be known as 'F' Entry; we would be the responsibility of one F/Sgt Fox (and a crafty one if ever there was), who would be assisted in his task by a corporal by the name of Jones (nicknamed "Pinhead" for no apparent reason).

First, we had to learn how to walk and march properly. I had been walking since I was a child, but it seems I had not been doing it properly. I have to admit, there was some cause for suspicion regarding some of the lads in our entry at the way they moved, but I suppose when you have been following assorted farm animals or a plough for the best part of your life, you are apt to wallow a little.

We were told that one always stepped off on the left foot and at the same time swung the right arm forward. This may appear quite natural to normal people, but surprisingly many of our entry moved both left arm and leg together at the same time, both forward and looking most odd, causing hoots of laughter – you try doing this! The problem appeared to be that some of us were not too sure which was left and which was right, this shortcoming was soon overcome when our instructor told us to put our hands out in front of us, palms downward. We should then open the thumb as far as possible and we would then see on the left hand we had formed an 'L' shape with the forefinger and thumb. We should now remember that was always the left! (there were not many 'O' Levels among this lot!).

Next we had to learn how to 'salute'. This was entirely different from anything we had done before. We had to carry out this manoeuvre using one hand and all four fingers, not just two as we had been used to doing! I am afraid some of the entry never really mastered this one and invariably gave the impression they were either waving goodbye to Mum, or saying 'so long' to their mates outside the railings. This of course, created other problems. We had to know just who we should salute and in their enthusiasm everyone in a peaked cap or wearing an unusual uniform was waved to and for a while many local tradesmen had their egos inflated.

One amusing episode relating to this occurred when one of our entry was walking near the headquarters building one day and passed without saluting one of the many Air Officers – an Air Commodore to be precise!

'Airman!' said a voice irately. 'Come back here.' Pointing to the thick gold ring on his sleeve he said, 'What do you think this is, FOG?' (an expression I am sure any ex-airman will appreciate), to which the shuddering airman replied, 'Well Sir… I saluted a man dressed like you yesterday but he turned out to be a United Dairies milkman who thought I was taking the Mickey out of him and threatened to do me over, so I didn't want to push my luck too far…'

The outcome was a few days 'jankers'.

Now followed endless drill sessions on the square where we were taught to march fast, slow, forwards and backwards – a routine which we followed for several months.

We were still confined to camp as we apparently looked a 'heap' in our uniforms and the only relief from the boredom, apart from the NAAFI, was the station 'cinema'. This was a single-storey building inside the station boundary to which the general public was admitted for a small fee – I think it was ninepence or one-and-threepence (old money). Wouldn't the IRA welcome that set-up today!

The cinema was managed by the RAF and in charge was one Sgt Icks, whose initials were 'F' for Fred and 'L' for Leslie and I have often wondered if the saying 'going to the Flicks' originated there, or was it because of the poor picture quality? To say they flickered would be an understatement. Sgt Icks was quite a character. He had been at Uxbridge for many years, no one knew how long, there were not many postings for cinema operators and managers in the RAF. He had started his service career as a 'wick trimmer second class', having failed the exam to become ACH/GD![1] Fortunately for him the present cinema had just opened as a 'magic lantern' house about the time he arrived on the station and there was a posting for a wick trimmer (I told you I did not know how long he had been in the service). He quickly realised that if he kept his lamp filled with oil and his wick clean and well trimmed he could keep this posting for life and from that moment on the Wise Virgins had nothing on him! He did remuster to Lamp Replacement Officer when the RAF replaced the

---

[1] Aircraft Hand General Duties.

magic lantern for a slide projector and when they progressed to 'movies' he was promoted to AVM – no, not that
kind – he was made an Audio and Video manager, second
class … unpaid and at times unwanted.

The other thing that happened to break the monotony of
just square bashing was my introduction to the airman's
best friend (?) – the rifle! By this time we were all fed up to
the teeth, had developed an intense hatred for the Flight
Sergeant and Corporal Jones was a marked man should we
ever go to war! Some wise guy must have appraised our
feelings, for we soon discovered that the firing pins had
been removed from our rifles and we would not be able to
shoot anyone! I did not realise that a rifle was for any other
purpose than for shooting someone or something, but our
instructor found others.

We carried the thing on alternate shoulders, across the
chest, at arms length, like a handbag and a movement 'rest
on your arms reversed'. Now for anyone of you who has
done this, you will know what comes next! In no time at all
there is an almighty noise as rifle after rifle hits the deck.
Rifles clatter to the ground, airmen fall over trying to grab
the errant one and no-one finishes up with the gun they
started with. It took about three weeks to get that one right.

Eventually things did fall into place as ordained and we
were drilling and marching in a very accomplished manner. By now, the expansion scheme had begun and there
were many more squads on the square and we began to
develop a competitive attitude and life became a little more
bearable.

4. The Opening Rounds

Before I proceed further with this chronicle, I would like to refer to an omission on my part from a previous chapter which concerns an item of kit called a 'swagger stick' or cane. This was a short, tapered stick about 20 inches long, black in colour and on the thick end was a chrome-plated knob about the size of a golf ball, embossed with the RAF crest. This would be carried tucked horizontally under the left arm with the knob facing forward and carried at all times when wearing 'best blue'. I refer to this only because of an interesting and astonishing happening concerning this item of kit. As I explained before, we recruits were a motley lot, sharing an assortment of dialects which at times, did create problems, as will be seen.

When we were eventually allowed passes to leave the station and go to town we had to wear 'best blue' and to present ourselves at the guard room for inspection. On this one special time I and four other lads duly presented ourselves and we were ordered, individually, by the duty corporal, who happened to speak with a broad Scottish accent, to what sounded very much like 'turnaboot'.

We were expected to polish not only the front of buttons, badges and belt brasses, but also the backs of these items and unfortunately the first of us to be ordered to 'turnaboot' was one Ginger Hodge, a cockney! Thinking that the Corporal had said 'turn the belt' he promptly turned his belt over for inspection. This was not what the corporal expected and after repeating the order several times and getting the same response each time, he said it once more and at the same time he pushed Hodge on his shoulder, wanting him to turn around, for this was what he was saying – 'turn about'! This was almost a fatal move on the corporal's part because Hodge slid his hand to the narrow end of his cane, raised it in the air and brought the knob down on the corporal's head as hard as he could. For a moment there was an awkward silence and I heard, for the first time, the order 'fall in two men'. Hodge was taken away, his kit was removed and we never saw him again. I don't know if an occurrence of this nature had ever happened before – I somehow don't think so – but I do know that we were the last entry to be issued with swagger sticks! I don't think the powers that be were going to take any further chances with such lethal weapons. Incidentally, if anyone has one of these canes or knows where there is one, it is worth a lot of money, hundreds, if not more.

We had now almost completed our nine months square bashing and I have to say we really were a very disciplined and competent squad. I can't help thinking what a wonderful exercise this could be for many of our tearaways of today. The day arrived for our Passing Out and as there were to be three entries involved, the AOC decided to witness the event. Our drill on the square went off perfectly and we were all delighted, then came the test on the rifle butts and here disaster struck! For this test we were issued with real serviceable rifles and ten rounds of live ammunition! Our squad were the first to go and we were given our specific target which were cut-outs of men (Germans of course).

For the first part of the exercise we were spread out in a line and had to advance towards the target with the rifle held in the 'port' position. (For the sprogs amongst you, this means the rifle is held across the front of the body with the right hand holding the butt and the left hand supporting the barrel). On the command 'prone' we were to drop to the ground; on the word 'fire' we were to let fly at the target. It had been decided that throughout the whole of the Passing Out, all instructions to the squad would be given by individual members chosen at random, the object being to assess the confidence and authority of the trainee; this had been part of our training and up to this point it had all gone off well, but…

Unfortunately, at this point the AOC had a wish to get in on the act and he selected the airman he would like to take charge of the rifle exercise. He chose a chap by the name of Stuart who came from Newcastle and who was one of the smartest on parade, but, regretfully he stuttered! To continue, we advanced on the target with the rifles at 'port' although some of the lads had them almost around their knees. The Drill Sergeant said to Stuart 'tell them to get their rifles up higher'; immediately Stuart said something like: 'Hu-Hup-Higher' and somebody pulled the trigger. From that moment all hell broke loose, the whole squad dropped to the ground, some on top of each other, bullets were flying everywhere. In the blinking of an eye, with the exception of the AOC and we members of the squad lying on the ground, the whole area was deserted. The AOC of course, had conjured up visions of an additional gong to the many already adorning his chest for standing firm in the face of hostile fire.

Many of the bullets had gone AWOL; the Town Hall Clock in Uxbridge stopped dead although it continued to strike the quarter hours non-stop for the rest of the day. The high church of St Mary prided itself on its magnificent stained glass windows and the gem of their collection was a whole panel depicting the nativity with Joseph leading a donkey with Mary on its back on the way to Nazareth. After the 'shoot out' Mary had taken off and was nowhere to be seen and Joseph was leading a headless mule! Several local gardeners were at a loss to know why panes of glass were missing from their greenhouses and until the facts leaked out put it down to constipated pigeons! Meanwhile, back at the barracks, it was decided to 'scrub' that part of the exercise and after reloading we completed our test on the rifle range without any further mishaps.

At the end of the day, we were all paraded on the square and thanked by the AOC for a very impressive performance (his words); he did not mention the shooting fiasco, perhaps 'impressive' covers it all. When our Drill Sergeant was asked by the AOC what he thought about his squad he replied he thought we could well give Adolph something to think about, to which the AOC answered 'you could well be right but one thing I can tell you, they put the fear of Christ into me!'

And so we could now put all the 'Bull' behind us and look forward to what the RAF is really all about – aeroplanes.

5. *Nearer, Mien Gott...*

Before I leave Uxbridge for the last time, I must tell of a happening that was to leave a profound effect on my attitude to service life, and the lesson learned was to stand me in good stead throughout my time in the RAF. As previously stated Uxbridge was then known as the Depot and as such had the very best in sporting facilities, a wonderful athletics stadium and a real super gymnasium. It was also conveniently situated on the outskirts of London and easily accessible, which is why so many service competitions were held there. There was also adequate accommodation for visiting teams. One such competition was the RAF boxing championships, which were to be held just as we were due to leave. However, two of my entry were taking part in this event, so we were kept back. It proved to be a successful week and the finals night was most enjoyable.

The next day, while we were idling our time away, awaiting further orders, we were visited by our drill Sergeant who, clipboard in hand, asked, 'Who wishes to be a pilot?' Almost to a man we put our names forward. The Sergeant, however, said he could only take twelve names and these would have to be the strongest and fittest among us. We lucky twelve were told to fall in outside and were marched to the gymnasium to be tested, or so we thought...

'Before we proceed further,' said the Sergeant, 'we have one small job to do..." And with that we were marched into the gym, which had been left as it was on the finals day of the boxing competition, with the ring in the centre surrounded by something like 1,500 chairs.

'What we have to do,' said the Sergeant, 'is move all these chairs. I want them stacked ten high at the end of the hall.' So, for the next four hours we did just that, by which time we were completely exhausted; it was no light task. When we had finished the Sergeant said we could make our own way back to our billets and thanked us for our efforts. When we asked him what moving all these seats had to do with being pilots he said in a very surprised voice, 'Pilot? I didn't say 'pilot' did I? I should have said 'PILER' and I must say you are the best pilers I have ever had!'

Perhaps it was just as well for all concerned that we left Uxbridge a few days after this episode and were taken to RAF Manston in Kent to join No. 3 School of Technical Training. At last we were beginning to feel much happier with service life, we had left much of the 'bull' behind and were learning how and why the RAF operated and actually started work on real aircraft.

This training period was to last almost eighteen months and I enjoyed every moment of it and learned an awful lot. Two happenings occurred during this period, the first being my introduction to flying (actually becoming airborne!) and the second was my involvement in the funeral of HM King George V (of which more in my next chapter).

At the time, in addition to No.3 SoTT, No.500 (County of Kent) Auxiliary Squadron was also based at Manston. This was a bomber squadron equipped with Vickers Virginia twin-engined aircraft. This was, at the time, the RAF's front-line bomber, successor to the well known 'Vimy', which had been so successful during the 1914/18 conflict. Both types were bi-planes, the Vimy powered by Rolls-Royce Eagle in-line engines, the Virginia by Napier Lion engines. Top speed was in the region of 100mph, flat out (some wag said they could only do this if the elastic was really wound up really tight!) We trainees were told that parties would be welcome on the squadron site to help with cleaning and in any other way we could. The reward would be the opportunity of an occasional trip, whenever possible. Needless to say there was no shortage of volunteers and being a keen type I grabbed any opportunity that came along.

Eventually the day came for me to go flying and much as I wanted to go I was somewhat apprehensive. You see, compared with today's aircraft the Virginia had a frightening aspect – it was painted black all over and really looked unsafe, almost as though it was about to break in two in the middle. I had read that this aircraft's predecessor, the Vimy, had been the first a/c to fly the Atlantic, west to east, piloted by Alcock and Brown. Reading further, it said that Brown had to walk out on the wings on six occasions to make some adjustments to the engines whilst it was flying!

I was asked if I would like to go 'up front' or would I like to go in the rear gunner's position? This called for a little thought. I kept thinking about 'wing walking' – at least I would be out of way in the 'tail'. I was also aware that aeroplanes did have a habit of flying into hills and mountains, but I had never read anywhere that a plane had reversed, knowingly, into a hill and so I reckoned I would be safer at the back! Of course, in those days there was no such thing as a 'black box' which, as we all know, is the only thing expected to survive a crash. Had there been one I should have chosen to sit on that! (My apologies here to Dave Gunston; these are actually his lines, I just put them in to brighten up an otherwise dull story!)

I was given an observer-type parachute complete with harness and told what I should do if I had to 'get out' before we landed 'officially'. I was then helped into the rear gunners compartment and held in by a single strap attached to the floor and a ring on my harness! The engines were then started and I found out what it is like sitting in the middle of a wind tunnel. As we moved off I thought I was going to be thrown out of my seat. This plane had nothing so sophisticated as a tail-wheel, just a solid bar of iron called a 'tail skid' and there were no runways in those days (I think the airfield had only just been ploughed).

And take-off was yet to come…

Suddenly all hell broke loose … the noise rose to a crescendo, the wind reached hurricane force and we were going like the clappers – but we were still on the ground and the boundary of the airfield was getting very close. I don't know where we were supposed to be going, but I did think just for a moment, that if the pilot had decided to go by road he ought to slow down a little.

Suddenly it was all peace and quiet and we were flying – and what a fantastic experience – but you all know about this. Luckily for me there were many more trips to come, but I don't think any were quite as exciting as the first.

6. The Dead and the Quick

The date is now January 1936 and I am about to be posted to my first real Air Force station – the Marine Aircraft Experimental Establishment (MAEE) at Felixstowe. This was a posting to which only the best were sent and my cap would not fit for quite a few days – then what happened? The 'boss man' up and died! I am referring, of course, to HM King George V, who died on January 20th 1936. There was mayhem in the ranks. We were now involved in a military state funeral and I had to take part, the reason for this being that my uniform, particularly my greatcoat, was new and also that I was still familiar with all the 'bull' – sorry, drill movements – which would be required for such an event. We had a short while to brush-up and then came the day of the event.

Although I cannot recall the actual day, I do know it was winter. Reveille was 2.30 am, breakfast at 3 am and we were loaded on to Leyland trucks at 3.30 am, by this time feeling very cold and wet. We were taken to Ramsgate station to be transported to Paddington station in London, where we were required to line the route of the procession via Praed Street. There was no direct line from Ramsgate to Paddington so we went through various shunting and by-passing manoeuvres (I am sure, at one time I saw a signpost that said six miles to Inverness!). Eventually, we finished up on each side of Praed Street, as planned, in all our glory, greatcoats, gloves, muskets and all, the time now being 6.30 am and it was raining! The street, even at that hour, was filled with people who had brought with them not only food to sustain themselves but food for the poor bloody troops as well who were lining the route. So for the next six to eight hours, all we heard was 'Hi soldier' (nobody was sure in those days just who was who), 'open up' and something was pushed into our mouths, sometimes it was liquid and sometimes solid – sometimes nice and sometimes horrid. Having imbibed all these goodies there came the time for one to want to go somewhere!

Now, I don't know what experience the RAF had of this type of operation, but somehow the 'bods' had to be relieved and with the help and advice of a couple of Air Marshals and the local lavatory attendant, it was arranged that we should number off – odds would go first and evens afterwards – and evacuate our positions in numerical order. Thus what could have been an embarrassing situation was overcome – but then the RAF could always rise to the occasion (*Per Adua Ad Astra*): remember the Battle of Britain, the Battle of the Bulge and Mafikeng? The latter, of course, was a relieving operation also!

Eventually the cortege entered our domain, the coffin was to be loaded onto the train at Paddington station and despatched elsewhere for burial and it was then that disaster struck. Remember, we had been at our post for almost 6 hours: it was wet and very cold. We were then ordered to 'slope arms' and then 'rest on the arms reversed'. For a few moments there was only the sound of heavy breathing followed by the sound of a house falling down; frozen fingers could not hold the butt of the rifle and the sound of rifles clattering on the road could well have been part of a Gershwin symphony. Fortunately our NCO in charge forgot all about his drill jargon and just said 'pick 'em up' and 'turn 'em upside down!' which we all did and eventually the cortege passed on its way and I think we even got admiring looks from some of the mounted mourners. This, I suppose was the last such state funeral, with all the crowned heads of Europe – and there were quite a few around at that time – apart from the potentates from India and the other colonies on display – a most impressive sight, I can assure you. Of course, in those days there was not a motor car in sight, everyone was mounted on horseback, even the gun carriage bearing the coffin was dragged by lots of sailors (not singing 'Yo Ho Ho! however').

I have wondered since about this pollution thing and although I know about cars being culprits, if you are standing anywhere near a large assortment of horses and they collectively decide to deposit heaps of '*umghali*' as they pass, literally at your feet, the end result (sorry about that one) is not pleasant and, as usual, there was not an 'environmentally friendly' person to be seen. At this point, I heard a Cockney voice behind me say, 'I told you Ethel, I should have brought my bucket and spade' and the reply from Ethel: 'you can pick up droppings anywhere Bert'. 'I know that,' says Bert, 'but this is Royal crap – I could have had the best rhubarb on the allotment!'

Finally the whole thing was over and the public dispersed. We were offered some refreshment, not that any of us really wanted food of any kind, having consumed the generous offerings of a caring public, the variety of which it would be difficult to explain and some, I may add, of a very dubious quality. I never did get the taste for sardine sandwiches together with strawberry ice cream and cheese crackers, all at the same time but from different sources.

And so we were returned to our unit in the same manner in which we had travelled to London, very tired, still very wet and thoroughly fed up, eventually arriving back at Manston at almost midnight.

Two weeks later, carrying all my worldly goods and my travel warrant, I was off to Felixstowe, to my first so-called operational station. I was pleasantly surprised at my reception on arrival, everyone was so friendly and helpful and I very soon felt at home. The station was situated on the southern bank of the river Orwell and had three very large hangers parallel to the river and about fifty yards from the river bank. In front of the centre hangar and mounted on a jetty was an enormous 'Hammerhead Crane' which could swivel through 190 degrees and was used to lift the giant flying boats out of the water, swing them around and lower them onto trolleys for transporting to the hangar. Spaced out and moored along the length of the river was a large assortment of flying boats and seaplanes, some were prototypes and others experimental or for modifications.

The manufacturers in those days classed their boats under the names of towns and cities of the world or they were given just a number e.g. Southampton, Perth, London, Singapore and the Sunderland which became the military version of the Empire Flying Boat. There was one exception to all these and this was a boat, which we called

'Knuckleduster' for reasons, I will explain later. On the station was also an operational squadron – No 209 – who were equipped with Singapores; these were bi-planes fitted with 2 x 2 in-line Rolls-Royce Kestrel engines, two pushing and two pulling, mounted between the upper and lower mainplanes. Overnight it seemed my life had been transformed, the work we were asked to do (note I said *asked*) was interesting and everyone was friendly; all NCOs from corporals upwards were helpful, all the 'bull' had gone, our food was excellent and there was plenty of it; it was just like it had been on 'civvy street'.

However, it was still winter and working on the boats out on the river could be cold and unpleasant. Of course, we each had to do our stints of guard duty, and it could get very cold and lonely patrolling the concourse and keeping a beady eye on the boats moored on the river – no one ever told us what to do if one should take off!

But, resourceful as ever, I did learn to knit! Not very successfully, I have to admit, but by the time I left Felixstowe, I did have a large assortment of woollen scarves with sleeves in them that nobody wanted! With the type of work we were doing, there was quite a lot of test flying carried out, which meant that there were many opportunities for the odd trip, which brings me to our dear 'Knuckleduster'. This was a very large flying boat, possibly the forerunner of the Empire boats and our first monoplane.

The problem with all flying boats and seaplanes was that, because they had to land and take off from water, which invariably was salty and corrosive, the engines had to be as high out of reach of the water as possible. The 'Knuckleduster' was some 10 feet in height and the mainplane mounted on top of the hull was also cranked upwards in what we now call a 'gull wing'. Two Rolls-Royce Goshawk engines were mounted on the 'knuckle' part of the wings, which meant that the engines were some 16 feet above the surface of the water. To keep the boat level in the water, floats were attached to the wing tips by very long struts. This arrangement worked very satisfactorily whilst the aircraft was on the water, but in flight was a different story: the floats started to oscillate on the ends of the struts and the wings literally fluttered; even at the lowest speed, inside the hull everything moved and so did I the first time I flew in the thing – and you will probably be able to guess in which direction! But it was very exhilarating and I was younger then and stupid (haven't changed much) but it has to be said that not many people opted to fly in this boat from choice.

The other frightening thing that occurred was when we flight tested a 'London' flying boat to which we had fitted 'stub planes' in place of the usual floats. As mentioned in the previous story, wing-tip floats had proved unsatisfactory because they created so much turbulence when the aircraft was in flight. Apparently the German Air Force (Luftwaffe) favoured these stub planes, which were, in effect, an additional small wing and provided extra lift, so the powers that be decided to go for them in a big way. Someone, somewhere made two sets of these stubs, a small and a large set and sent them to us, together with fitting instructions (you think D.I.Y. is something new?) and soon we got down to the task of attaching the things. To do this we had to have the boat out of the water and after a week of tinkering we had finished the job and were ready to try them out.

Nothing was going to keep me off the test flight. Take off was normal, in fact we seemed to get up much quicker and smoother than usual. We flew around for about an hour and then prepared for approach and landing. The London usually came in at about 80-90 mph, depending on whether the pilot had had his lunch or not, and this time we followed the same procedure. Usually we hit the water with a slight thud and then aquaplaned until we came to a stop, just bobbing in the water.

Not this time! We seemed to touch down quite smoothly but then began to emulate a submarine. I didn't remember hearing anyone say 'Dive, dive, dive!' but we did just that. We came from 80 mph to a dead stop (shouldn't have used that word really) in a few moments and some 10 feet un-derwater. Everyone went a shade of green and for the first time ever the pilot and navigator found the remaining nine occupants of the plane in the cockpit alongside them – rather 'chummy' don't you think? – together with anything else that was not bolted to the floor. For the first time, ever, I saw fishes swimming above me instead of below. There was an awful lot of blood around and some of it was mine, but thankfully none of my bones were broken. Others were not so lucky and there was a lot of moaning.

By this time we had come to the surface and were intent on getting off. Our pilot, one Flt/Lt Flemming, was about forty years of age and suffered with gout; all he kept on saying was 'This is not going to do my bloody gout any good at all!'

Rescue workers were very quickly on the scene and we were all taken ashore to the sick bay immediately. Apart from the odd broken limb sustained by a few of us, we all luckily survived what could have been a possibly fatal accident. Luckily, before I had the opportunity to try my luck with the other set of stub planes, I was posted to No. 802 Squadron of the Fleet Air Arm, based at Lee-on-Solent...

7. A Naval Interlude

During the short period I was at Felixstowe I really began to enjoy service life; the only real problem was that we were always so short of money – we were only paid ten shillings per week, out of which we had to make an allowance home of two and sixpence! The solution to this problem was to get ones feet 'under the table' somewhere – and Yours Truly was very lucky in this respect. At a dance one evening I met 'Donna' – a girl of Italian descent whose father (Papa) owned and ran a café on the seafront where the family also lived. Of course a 'brave airman' was welcomed into the home with open arms and from then on I was never short of a good meal. Donna was also quite satisfying (you know what these Latins are!) Whilst I was at Felixstowe I passed as an L.A.C. (Leading Aircraftman) and when I turned up at the Café Minori with my 'props' sewn in place, Papa saluted me, laid on a six-course meal and told all and sundry that his Donna was going out with the 'Lord of the Air Corps' – that's how he interpreted L.A.C.!

And then, just when I had begun to enjoy visions of a villa in Minori – a wonderful part of Italy – and everything looking just fine – what happens? I get posted! Sadly I said goodbye to Felixstowe and farewell to my Donna; I wasn't sure what I would miss the most, her, or the spaghetti!

I arrived at Lee-on-Solent to be informed that the squadron was about to embark for a cruise through the

Mediterranean on the aircraft carrier HMS *Courageous* – which didn't sound too bad to me. Two days after I had arrived I was told that the squadron's aircraft would be flying out to the carrier, which was cruising somewhere in the western approaches to the English Channel, and that most of the ground staff were already on board. The squadron was equipped with the Fairey Swordfish, affectionately known as the 'Stringbag' – thin struts, fabric covered and literally held together with string – but a lovely aircraft to fly in. When it was suggested that I could fly out to the carrier in one of the planes, I jumped at the chance. My pilot was to be a Sgt Forbes, who was very friendly but who, I thought, eyed me with tolerance, sympathy and some amazement. He, of course, knew what was in store for me as a 'new boy'.

Take off was smooth, quiet and after Virginias of 500 Squadron, marvellous. We flew for about 30 minutes and then the pilot said, 'There's Mum down there... let's drop in for a cup of tea!' I looked where he was pointing and saw what appeared to be a leaf floating on the water – it was so tiny. I don't know what our altitude was, but I now feel I have an affinity with the astronauts when they look at the earth from the surface of the moon and know that is where they have to return to! I think I gulped a few times and said to the pilot, "Do we *have* to land on that leaf down there? Wouldn't it be more sensible to go back to Lee-on-Solent and land, then wait for the carrier to come and fetch us?'

He didn't seem to be very interested. 'Don't worry,' he said, 'it will be fine!' I closed my eyes, said a few 'Hail Marys' and hoped for the best...

After what seemed about 10 years, there was an almighty bump, a great hissing sound and what appeared to be an attempt to throw me out of the plane before I had released my harness. We had landed – and all in one piece – and after having put back everything that had come loose (with, of course, one exception!) I left the aircraft and for the first time, found myself on the deck of a warship.

We were on course for Gibraltar and for the next few days I was initiated into the wonderful ways and mysteries of life in the Royal Navy. We no longer slept in beds but emulated the shape of bananas in hammocks which were slung between hooks about eight feet above the wooden mess deck. Turn over in the night and, likely as not you would be off to the sick bay with multiple injuries. I very quickly learned what it meant to 'lie doggo'.

We integrated with the naval ratings, living and eating together on our individual mess deck, which accommodated 12 to 18 men. We were given a messing allowance: food was purchased from the quartermaster and prepared and cooked by navy personnel who had received training in this field – and quite successful it all was. Eventually we arrived at Gibraltar where we were to be joined by the *Ark Royal*, the battleship HMS *Barham* and others. Then came another change of plans. Unknown to me, a civil war had been going on in Spain and some dirty deeds were taking place in the Mediterranean which were not acceptable by either us or the French. A meeting between the two countries was held in Lyon, France and it was decided to set up an air patrol to keep 'tabs'. This would entail two squadrons of flying boats supplied by the RAF and based on French territory in Algeria, no so numbers 209 and 210 Squadrons operating with Short Singapore flying boats together with their servicing personnel were sent on their way. The base from which they were to operate was at a place in Algeria name Arzew, some 25 miles east of Oran.

Meanwhile, I and about 12 other airmen had been ordered to leave the carrier and were transferred to a submarine repair ship in Gibraltar harbour – and what was this little beauty called? – HMS *Cyclops* – known affectionately throughout the Royal Navy as 'that one-eyed bastard'. This ship had been borrowed from the RN and was to be our base and our home and would be moored in Arzew bay. The ship was very old and had originally been used to carry meat from Argentina before it was purchased by the Royal Navy. It would appear that the 'Argies' left tons of bully beef on board when they flogged this ship because it seemed we ate nothing but bully beef for the next six months! I seem to remember that every time I passed a cow in a field she would nod to me! However, our *Cyclops* had one saving grace; she had fabulous workshops aboard, including a floating surface table and machines galore.

We finally docked in Arzew, against a large jetty which protruded out into what was known as 'Crystal Bay'. This jetty was some 50ft wide and about 200ft long. There was a heavy duty mobile crane with which we were able to lift our boats out of the water onto peaching trolleys. Arzew was a small Algerian seaside resort with an enclosed bay which really was crystal clear and our boats were moored in this bay. Eventually when we came to work on these aircraft whilst afloat, it happened that the odd tool would be dropped overboard and although moored in about 20ft of water it was no problem to dive down and retrieve, in fact I think many tools were thrown in on purpose – somewhat different from working conditions at Felixstowe!

It has always surprised me that with the post war development of holiday resorts in the Mediterranean, Arzew has never been considered with Oran so near and Algiers a little further away, together with many other interesting places. I would have thought it a 'natural'.

Living conditions on board were more complicated than on the *Courageous*; for starters, there were now 30 men on a mess and we still all had to sleep in hammocks over the mess deck. Everyone went to bed (ha ha) at the same time and this was a very carefully executed manoeuvre because if a bod did not get himself wedged in at the start, he spent the night lying on the mess deck – which was very hard. Nobody went to the 'head' during the night – he wouldn't dare, for one thing, and he couldn't for another – unless he pushed the side of the ship out. Being 'on the bottle' had an entirely different meaning on our boat!

Eating on board was one more problem for us all. We had no Naval personnel to guide us. We were given an allowance for food and to each mess deck was appointed an ACH who would *do* for us (and very nearly did!). The drill was that we formed a messing committee who decided what we would eat, arrange for our ACH, whom we christened 'Dizzy' (and this fitted him perfectly) to collect from the store and do what preparation was required, take it to the galley to be cooked and then collect when we came on board after work. It did not work out very well; nothing ever looked or tasted as it should have done, but strangely enough our Dizzy did get quite good at making pastry, so we lived on sausagemeat, corned beef and camel meat (?). It was all covered with pastry – vegetables were non-existent but rice was in abundance.

The only other meat we had came with the breakfast – it was called 'porridge' but the weevils outnumbered the oats and so it was what you might call a meat dish – and the first time I ever saw anyone shake Daddy's sauce onto porridge!

We were provided with various cooking utensils, among which was an enormous teapot made of aluminium which looked more like a large coal scuttle but could hold enough tea for us all. We were restricted to just two gallons of water per person each day for drinking, cooking and washing (pass the Chanel No 5 please!) and a 10 gallon container was given to each five persons to share, which necessitated a log being kept. It all worked out fairly well; for example when making tea Dizzy would put in the amount of tea required and then take the pot to the galley where they would put in the amount of hot water required and deduct that amount from our next issue.

There was one amusing incident relating to this exercise which came about after we had been on board for about a week. One morning, at breakfast, our corporal picked up the teapot and there was very little tea left, which was strange because there was usually plenty for all. And yet the pot felt quite heavy, which made the corporal peer inside. With that he took hold of a wash bowl, tipped the teapot upside down and out fell a huge heap of cooked cock-roaches mixed up with a week's supply of tea leaves!

Apparently our Dizzy had just put more tea in each day without cleaning out the pot. The cockroaches must have crawled in during the day, seeking warmth, and drowned when the new batch of hot water was added. And we had been blaming the RN for stocking inferior tea! After that there was an inspection each day.

Somehow we survived all these hardships. It was a new adventure for most of us, the work was interesting and we had plenty of leisure time, swimming was fabulous and what night life there was – all very enjoyable. Regrettably the operation only lasted a few months, quite futile I think, and nobody seemed to know what was to follow. We were allowed to arrange trips and outings to places around of interest and this was really great.

One trip we all wanted to go on was to Sidi bel Abbas, the home of the French Foreign Legion. These headquarters were situated at the foothills of the Atlas Mountains some 50 miles south of Oran, but we were told it could be dangerous going to 'Sidi' as the whole area was infested by hostile Arabs and Bedouins and certain precautions must be taken. And here I must tell those of you who are not initiated, about the 'goolie chit' and this is not to be taken with a pinch of salt (sorry, I am getting my metaphors mixed up again), it is all perfectly true...

I had heard about this from many airmen who had served time in the Gulf or the Canal Zone and the issue of these chits came about as follows. The whole of that area at that time was swarming with hostile Arabs who particularly disliked the British, whose aircraft unfortunately quite frequently force-landed in hostile territory and had to be rescued. It was a disgraceful and objectionable custom at that time that should any British serviceman be captured by any of these Arabs he would immediately be handed over to the women of the tribe. Now it appears that these 'ladies' were very partial to testicles and their unfortunate captives would very swiftly be relieved of theirs. Perhaps these 'goodies' had aphrodisiac qualities or just made tasty sandwiches! Anyway, this was of great concern to the service chiefs (the poor bloody captives were not very happy either!) but it was discovered that these womenfolk would look even more favourably on a few extra 'akkers' and so the 'goolie chit' came into being... It was an orange coloured document with a photo of the bearer and other relevant details and stated (in Arabic) that in exchange for the safe and 'intact' return of the person described, whoever had ensured this return would be rewarded with a sum of money. It worked, I know, because I am still intact! It was, therefore, greeted with some surprise and a little trepidation when a similar document was issued to all of us at Arzew. I had thought this particular hazard was confined to the Gulf area but, apparently, the gastronomic delights of the ladies of Arabia were also shared with their sisters in Algeria – so out of the wallet went the passport and in went the 'goolie chit'.

Unfortunately this great adventure ended all too soon; the whole operation only lasted about eight months, but I did have a wonderful time. It was now almost Christmas 1937 and everyone was hoping to be home for the occasion; my big fear was that I would be returned to the carrier to rejoin the Fleet Air Arm – a prospect I was not looking forward to. We sailed in *Cyclops* to Gibraltar and were billeted in Casemates barracks for the night. Early the following morning we were told to assemble on the dockside with all our kit. Moored up to the dock was a beautiful liner – the P&O ship *Kaiser and Hind* and we were told to 'pick up your parrots and monkeys, stop crying in the rear rank and move up the gangplank smartly!'

We did not need telling twice. I didn't completely relax until we had set sail, after which I felt safe and just began to wonder what was in store for me next…

8. Another Interlude

You will recall in my last episode I was about to take my leave of Gibraltar and mentioned that I, and the others, only stayed on the Rock overnight; this was not so, we actually spent about three days there. This allows me to tell you of my impressions of Gibraltar at that time and about one ludicrous occurrence that befell me. The Rock at that time was inhabited by wealthy Spaniards hiding from Franco, well-to-do English gentry hiding from the Inland Revenue, an assortment of dubious characters hiding from Customs and Excise, plus several service-wallahs hiding from the Red Caps. It really was a 'bolt-hole' on a grand scale. All booze and cigarettes were duty free, there was no income tax, in fact there did not seem to be a tax on anything, but they were a patriotic lot, for there were union flags everywhere. The place was coloured red on all the maps and nobody was going to rock the boat!

I do not recall too much about my short stay on the Rock but I remember very well my day spent in the town. Along with several other airmen, I visited a few of the places of interest; we then tried a few of the bars and for some unexplained reason found ourselves in a cinema. No... it was not showing 'blue' movies, just some romantic trash featuring an actor named Raymond Navarro, who was very popular at that time. He appeared to be dressed for most of the film in a very sexy pyjama suit known at the time as a

'Cossack style' – kind of double-breasted and fitting close around the neck. Dressed in this fashion he spent most of the film chasing all kinds of women about the place – with a remarkable degree of success.

Upon leaving the cinema we visited the local outdoor market, which comprised an assortment of stalls selling all kinds of goods and produce all manned and run by Spaniards of both sexes. One stall we came to was selling shirts, socks, pyjamas, etc, the owner being a very large Spanish Senora who displayed the most enormous pair of boobs I had seen up to that time! To say I was overawed would be an understatement. Being the true son of a greengrocer the thought immediately went through my mind, 'you wouldn't get many of those to a pound'! However, my eyes finally moved to where the pyjamas were on display and lo-and-behold, there was a sexy suit just like the one I had seen in the recent film. I'm not sure whether it was because of the film or that well-endowed Spanish saleslady – but the thought crossed my mind that such a garment might possibly work the same magic for me as it had done for that Navarro chap – remember I was at an impressionable age and the 'birds' had been a little thin on the ground of late! And so I bought a pyjama suit, even though the only one of my size was purple in colour!

I took my prized purchase back to the barracks and the evening could not come soon enough for me to try it on. There were about thirty other men in our room and suddenly I was aware that they were all looking in my direction. I very quickly dived under the blanket; I did not want anyone to get any funny ideas! I think I did sleep the night unmolested – I say this because I awoke in the morning to find myself as naked as the day I was born and the bed full of assorted pieces of purple material! I had to convince myself that this was due to the fact that I was sleeping in a strange bed and had been restless in the night! You can well imagine the leg pulling and the comments that were made. I did not take the offending article back. I think I would have been too embarrassed and anyway I think we were under orders to sail next day.

The *Kaiser-and-Hind* was in no way a cruise liner. She was a first-class only vessel and we were all amazed that we would be allowed to sail on her. She was used regularly on the Far East run for transporting tea planters, politicians justifying their existence, civil servants, military top brass, opium dealers and an assortment of other dubious characters, all very wealthy and many eyes were raised when we all trooped aboard. We were, however, confined to the stern area of the ship which was roped off and patrolled by service police at all times. There was one further stop before we really set sail for England and this was when we dropped anchor in Tangiers harbour to allow the passengers to do a little shopping – and a most enterprising exercise this turned out to be, as I will tell in my next chapter.

I have never since visited Gibraltar although I did get very close on a couple of occasions. The first was during the war – I was on board the S.S. *Franconia* en route for the Middle East to take part in the invasion of Sicily. At that time the Straits of Gib was no place to dawdle or sightsee and in true naval tradition we passed through the Straits like the proverbial 'dose of salts', many of us saying a few 'Hail Marys' as we did so.

The second occasion was some 12 years later – well after the war had ended – and because we had been victorious, although we were still on some form of rationing such as petrol coupons, we would be allowed to travel abroad providing we did not take more than £50 out of the country! And so my friend and I and our two wives (just one each!) decided to investigate Spain – perhaps in my case a sneaking desire to see that curvaceous Spanish lady again, or someone with similar qualifications.

I was, at that time, the proud owner of an Austin A40, in which we did duly journey forth – not a very large car and not too comfortable for four people but very easy to push (a sensible consideration when petrol was in short supply or non-existent). We did not book any accommodation in advance but just motored until we decided to stop – or the car did – and then looked for digs. I can assure you that £50 did not go very far, although everything in Spain was very cheap at that time. If it had not been for the odd and unexplained finding of a few notes or two in out-of-the-way pockets and crevices of ones apparel, I am sure we would all have finished up doing the washing up in some out-of-town Spanish bistro!

We eventually found ourselves in a small coastal resort south of Marbella and on consulting the map we realised that we were not far from Gibraltar and decided to patronise the Rock and donate them a few of our remaining pesetas. This was not to be, however, for along the way we were stopped by an unsavoury bunch of Spanish militia, all armed to the teeth and quite hostile. I don't know who they belonged to; they all wore a nondescript uniform surmounted by a black hat, a type of boater. All, it would appear, had walked into a door, for their hats were turned upwards in the front to be at 90 degrees to the rest of the brim – an odd looking lot.

Of course, we English were amazed that not one of them could speak our language and were at a loss to explain to them that the war had ended some ten years ago and that we had won! Their leader, an ugly brute of a man, asked for what sounded like 'cig'. Everyone smoked in those days and we all offered. They took every packet we had and also our passports and were still not very friendly. We were becoming just a little concerned. We were, after all, miles from anywhere on a road (if that's what you could call it) that could in no way be mistaken for the M25. It was what might be termed 'a dodgy situation'.

At this point my pal's wife, with the intuition bestowed only upon the fair sex, dived into her handbag (perhaps not a smart thing to do with an armed foreign gorilla standing just a few feet away), brought out a bag of sweets and said, "Would anyone care for a bullseye?"

I have thought of this moment recently with all the talk about 'Mad Cow' disease and wondered if this was where it started! But it did the trick; they very quickly took all the sweets we had, with almost the semblance of a smile. They would not, however, allow us to continue with our journey, and made us turn around, which we promptly did. They gave us back our passports and waved us goodbye – and so, once again I had failed to revisit Gibraltar.

9. *Circuits and Bumps*

You will recall that in my last chapter I mentioned that after we had left Gibraltar and before we really set sail for the UK we stopped over at Tangiers for a shopping spree; this was apparently a customary undertaking for most homeward bound liners. The ship did not actually dock but just dropped anchor in the bay to allow the local traders to market some of their wares. These 'goodies' comprised quite an assortment of items ranging from wood carvings to leather goods and skins, carpets and curtains, redundant wives and offspring and all the usual native paraphernalia. These goods were transported out to the liner on board some of the most primitive craft I had ever seen, heavily loaded as you can imagine and many already taking on water. When these boats reached the liner, the merchants heaved a line up to the deck on which we were all standing and attached to the other end of the line was a basket filled with the goodies. These were then hauled aboard, examined and a possible purchase made, after which the basket was pulled back below with any unwanted goods and payment for anything retained, and here the fun started.

Most of the 'customers' were so-called upper class, who one expected to play by the rules and in most cases were honourable and generous in making their payments. What the locals below did not know was that 'our mob' was aboard and that there were not many 'akkers' between the lot of us! What we did have, however, was an assortment of 'washers' which had worked very well for us in various cigarette and slot machines! Why not here? We were also well endowed with a thing called a 'Batchelor Button' – a type of press-stud fastener very popular at the time and used by servicemen to obviate having to sew on buttons. This form of payment did, however, cause some consternation among the ranks down below! Some thought that a new form of currency had arrived on the scene whilst others did not look very pleased at all and voiced their objections accordingly. Some even fell into the sea! Bedlam reigned for a while. We were, of course, quite safe from any physical objections, being some twenty or thirty feet beyond their ire, but nevertheless we were happy when we upped anchor and sailed for home.

And so we proceeded without further incident until we arrived in the UK and docked at Tilbury on December 23rd 1937 to be greeted by Custom and Excise. We were taken to the cleaners over our acquisitions from the 'Tangier Traders', either we paid duty on what we had or we could throw them in the sea, which quite a few of us did, after all, a new packet of 'buttons' was not that costly. We were then notified of our new posting.

I feared I would be posted back to the Fleet Air Arm or hopefully back to Felixstowe but my posting was to No.3 Flying Training School at Grantham and with it came a railway warrant to get me there. I eventually made my way there, arriving around tea-time, only to be told that 3FTS had moved out to a place called South Cerney in Gloucestershire and that is where I now had to go. They did, however, feed and house me until the next day and however, feed and house me until the next day and then sent me off in the direction of South Cerney. I began to wonder whether the King at the time or any of his cronies like the local AOC were trying to get a message across to me! I had already been posted to one squadron and found myself on a battleship and then promptly taken off this and posted to the 'OEB' (remember Cyclops?). I just wondered what was in store for me now, little did I know that I was to be almost carried out with my boots on!

But, wonder of wonders, this turned out to be a great posting – a new aerodrome, very good quarters and excellent food. It was one of four other aerodromes set up in this area for training pilots; someone obviously had some idea of what was in store. A scheme was put into operation called a 'Short Service Commission', where suitable applicants would be offered a six-year term of service provided that they could pass the required training to become operational aircrew. The scheme attracted a wide range of applicants from many walks of life, both from home and overseas; some could be called 'gentlemen' and were so in every way, others were of a more dubious character!

For the first time I associated and worked with men (and boys) helping to train them for what the Royal Air Force was really all about – defending the country when needed. I got to know many of them fairly well and have often wondered just how many of these lads survived the war. I did hear of a few who did not.

It was a great year for me despite the fact that there was a lot of hard and tiring work. As you can imagine, the aircraft took an awful lot of punishment and there were one or two bad and sad incidents. There were quite a few 'hairy' moments too – and not just for the pupils, especially when we were on night flying.

The landing strip (there were no concrete runways in those days) was marked out by things called 'goose neck flares', which some of you will be familiar with. This was a contraption much like a watering can filled with paraffin; a piece of cloth was pushed into the spout to soak up the oil. They were spaced out at intervals and (hopefully) ignited but were promptly blown out every time a pupil landed and had to be relit very quickly ready for the next pupil, our salvation (and theirs) depending upon a box of matches and our fleetness of foot – 'tough luck mate' if it was raining!

There were opportunities for participation in all kinds of sports and I promptly joined the station swimming team. Most other team members were officer pupils and we really did have an outstanding water polo team. Our captain was one of our pupil pilots and every ounce a gentleman. One of the things he introduced us to was a way to overcome our opponents. He gave us half a Spanish onion each to eat before a match and once in the water we were soon 'belching' like mad. If one of our opponents came anywhere near us we faced them and belched, whereupon they would turn in horror and we would be off like a shot. Only a 'gentleman of character' could come up with such a ploy; we did, however, win a lot of matches and could have put many Arab Sheiks to shame!

We had a motley selection of aircraft to operate: for *Ab Initio* training we used Tiger Moths, Tutors and later Magisters. For advanced flying we had Hawker Variants, Harts,

Hinds, Desmonds, Audaxs and Furys. I once flew in an Audax during an open day as passenger, my observer-type chute stowed away as instructed and anchored to the floor by a very thin piece of webbing and attached to my harness. Halfway through the display my pilot turned our plane upside down and guess what? No, I did not fall out, but I said goodbye to a perfectly good pair of pants!

It was usual before the day's flying program began, for several of the instructors to carry out weather checks or test fly serviced aircraft and there were many opportunities to go flying. It was on one of these test flights that I came a cropper! I had become very friendly with one of our instructors, Flg/Sgt Jenkins, who was also in our swimming team. On this particular morning he was to test a Tiger Moth on which I had been working and asked me if I would like to go along. I jumped at the chance, because on many previous occasions he had allowed me to take over the controls and had taught me quite a lot about flying. One manoeuvre he had shown me and which I found very thrilling was 'side slipping', used to lose height. On this occasion we had been flying for about 30 minutes when 'Jenks' decided we had had enough and said, "Let's go home". He had allowed me to pilot the plane quite a bit, but I was surprised when he asked, 'Fancy trying a landing?'

Carefully guiding me all the time, we approached the airfield and he remarked that I was too high. 'Slip it, slip it,' he said, and I think I gave it 'right stick and right rudder' as he had taught me.

There is a saying for when things are not as they should be – 'someone has moved the goalposts' but on this particu-

lar day someone must have moved the perimeter fence ...
because we hit it! I really thought the world had come to an
end; there was an awful, violent, tearing noise, terrific
vibrations and all kinds of things flying around, including
Yours Truly. Then it was almost quiet. I was upside down,
still held in by my harness, with my head among the clover
and peering through the gap between the rim of the cockpit and the ground and seeing lots of 'bods' racing across
the airfield to get to us. I was not aware of any panic, I knew
that I was still alive and had no pain but I was conscious of
a strong smell of petrol and could hear a sound like running water and realised that we had punctured the petrol
tank. I then began to feel a little apprehensive, but fortunately our rescuers had reached us and happily the Tiger
Moth is a very light aircraft and they were able to lift the
tail section and get us both out.

The aircraft did not appear to be too badly damaged and
neither Flt/Sgt Jenkins or myself appeared to be injured.
We were, however, loaded on the 'blood wagon' and carted
off to sick bay for a check-up. We were both excused all
duties for a week, except for making statements about the
crash but at the subsequent Court of Enquiry the officiating
officers would not accept Jenks's excuse that his pet gremlin
had snatched the controls out of his hand or that 'he' may
also have moved the perimeter fence. They decided it was
due to a sudden crosswind and he got off with a reprimand.
No blame was attached to me but I was, however, posted
from the unit a few weeks later. And where do you think I
was posted to? Yes, you are right, 615 Squadron, Kenley,
just down the road from where I lived.

10. Kenley 1938

I was about to take my leave of No.3 FTS and as was customary I did my rounds with the inevitable 'chit' – everything in those days was covered by a 'chit' of one kind or another (remember the 'goolie' one?) – this particular one was a 'clearance chit'.

It had been put around some time in the past by an ominous 'Devil Dodger' that one came into the world with nothing and therefore nothing could one take out. Now the RAF went for this in a big way and instituted the 'clearance chit' whereby any person being posted from a unit would visit every section involved with operating the unit, i.e. Transport, Medical, Messing, Armoury etc, the object being that they did not want anyone sneaking off with the odd 3-tonner, a supply of drugs, an aircraft or two, or a crate of hand grenades, and I think it did cut a little of that sort of thing down. What had not occurred to the top brass was that any 'erk' or DIY enthusiast had already built his own car, added an extension to his house and possibly built his own boat, all with a little help from 'Main Stores' and 'Station Workshops'!

Finally, I surrendered my completed 'chit' to my Flight Commander, who informed me that due to my experience with Hawker aircraft I was being posted to a Squadron who were flying that type of machine. He wished me well, said how sorry he was to see me go and what a big help I had been, but he did not shake my hand (perhaps because while making his speech he had the fingers of both hands tightly crossed behind his back!).

As I left South Cerney, little did I know that some 25 years later, I should be followed by my son, who would be posted here for initial Officer training.

And so I made my way to RAF Kenley to join 615 Auxiliary Squadron who were flying Hawker aircraft (joke over!) and I did not make a very good start. My train pulled into Kenley station and after watching it depart the stationmaster, standing nearby, looked at my kitbag and uniform and said 'are you for Kenley aerodrome?'. On my answering 'Yes' he said, 'You have got out at the wrong station. You want the next station down the line, Whiteleafe, there is another train in about 2 hours.'

Thanking him for this kind information, I asked that as I was at Kenley station could I not walk to the camp? He turned round and pointed to a range of mountains in the distance and said, 'It's up there somewhere. You'd be better off going to Whiteleafe.'

So I sat it out and eventually caught the next train to Whiteleafe, a station I had passed two hours ago. Here I was told how to find Whiteleafe Hill and told that I should climb to the top and look for Salmonds Lane and that the airfield would be 'somewhere about'! It was December, it was snowing (winter had come early that year) and they had not told me at the station that a supply of crampons and an ice pick would have been useful! With difficulty I pushed on, constantly thinking of the RAF motto and humming 'Excelsior' to myself all the while. I did pass a couple of natives going downhill but they were obviously not 'Sherpas', which is what I needed, so I just pushed on. Then, through the mist I saw the summit and that someone had planted a flag there – someone had obviously been here before! Staggering on further I recognised the RAF Standard and realised I had arrived at the airfield. There, in front of me, was the familiar Guard Room; why do they all look alike?

I very soon settled in and was taken the next day to the hangar to meet my Flight Commander and Flight Sergeant who would explain to me what was involved in working with an auxiliary squadron and I would also get a look at the aircraft I would be working on. I was told that the squadron had been formed as an Army Co-operation outfit and supplied with Hawker Audax and Hector aircraft. This had, however, now been changed, and we were to be equipped with Gloster Gauntlet aircraft – so much for my Hawker training! At this particular moment the squadron had two Tiger Moths, two Avro Tutors, one Hawker Hector and an assortment of Gauntlets. Given my experience, I was allocated the Hector to care for, a type I had never seen before and which would be leaving us shortly.

Now the Hector was the odd one out of the Hawker family, being powered by a Napier Dagger engine instead of the usual Rolls-Royce Kestrel – and what a giant of an engine this Dagger was! 24 cylinders in a letter 'H' configuration, two banks of six cylinders upright and two banks of six upside down.

Aero engines in those days were not the easiest things to get started; push starting was out of the question, but for medium aircraft we did a thing called hand swinging (highly dangerous for the poor bloke holding the prop). Then we had a system called 'cartridge firing', where an explosive cartridge was used; the explosive gasses would force the cylinders to move and the engine would (hopefully) start – a somewhat frightening procedure. And then there was the (death defying) 'Huck Starter' – a Heath Robinson contraption mounted on a tractor with a projecting rod which engaged with what was known as a 'dog' attached to the boss of the airscrew. With the Hector I was to learn yet another way, known as 'inertia starting', which involved a flywheel weighing about a ton (that's what it felt like anyway) attached to the engine through a clutch mechanism; when revolving like the clappers it could be engaged with the engine, turning it over and hopefully starting it – that was the theory, anyway. Now, to get the flywheel moving one was supplied with a starting handle (your grandfather will tell you what this looked like) which you pushed into the innards of the engine compartment where indicated and then emulated an Italian Organ Grinder (your grandfather will tell you about these too), winding the handle like mad.

You were not supplied with a stepladder or a platform of any kind to carry out this function; you positioned your left foot on the nearby landing wheel, your right leg bent at the knee, and somehow placed it on the leading edge of the lower mainplane. At the same time to keep you in place you wound your left arm around the nearest mainplane strut and now looked like the Organ Grinder's Monkey! Now you would start turning like mad. After a short, but

what seemed like a long period everything started to shake
– the aircraft because of the ton of iron whizzing around
and you because of the exertion! You now pulled on a ring
which said 'pull' (they thought of everything) which was
connected to the clutch mechanism; the propeller moved
to a different position, there was a strange clanking sound
and then came a noise like an expiring overweight duchess
followed by ... silence! So 'off we go' again!

Fortunately, at about this time the re-equipping of the
squadron began in earnest and we said goodbye to Hector.
Mind you, there was another reason, I think – the hernia
rate for ground staff was going through the roof!

With the arrival of the Gauntlets there came yet one
more way of starting engines. This was the 'Battery Starter
Trolley' – a large wooden box slung between a pair of
wheels, with a long handle to pull the thing around, very
much like a kid's go-cart and possibly where the idea came
from. The box was packed full of electric batteries, coupled
together to provide a very powerful charge, connected to a
heavy-duty cable with a plug at the end, which was inserted
into a socket on the aircraft; through co-ordinated signals
between pilot and ground crew, buttons were pressed and
the engine started almost always.

This method was a great boon to the ground staff but in
the early days turned out to be somewhat hazardous for the
pilot, who, having successfully started the engine, would be
slowly taxiing onto the runway only to hear a gentle
'thump, thump, thump'. This would mean that the ground
crew had left the battery lead still plugged in and that the
starter trolley was about to take off with him! The ground

crew were also in the habit of draping the cable across the mainplane, where it would snag up around a strut or flying wire with the same result. Under these circumstances the pilot would be well advised not to attempt to take off – given that these trolley starters were not aerodynamically designed and did not fly at all well (I don't think I ever heard of one getting a certificate of airworthiness). This problem was overcome very quickly (surprising what a spell of 'jankers' will do) and as the Air Ministry were considering going over to monoplanes at about this time, perhaps this hurried them along in their decision – with monoplanes there were not so many bits and pieces to hang things on.

Before leaving the subject of battery starters it occurred to me whilst writing this episode that full merit has never been given to this piece of equipment and the idea behind it. I am convinced that, but for this method of starting aero engines, we would never have won the Battle of Britain or even the war itself; Jerry would have been over and back before we had the 'Huck' out of the way and as for the thought of using it to launch a 'thousand bomber raid'... it would have taken a week to get them airborne! Well done kids! I now know why the 'Hundred Year's War' took such a long time – they did not have battery starters!

11. Up To The Starting Gate

I soon made friends with many of the regular airmen with whom I would be living and working and they quickly explained what it was like to be working on an Auxiliary squadron; it seemed much like any other squadron except it entailed always working at weekends with Tuesdays and Wednesdays off in lieu. I was aware at the time of a somewhat resentful attitude among the regular airmen, not so much towards the auxiliary airmen but more towards the pilots, who seemed to treat it all as a private flying club.

Our week started on Monday, repairing the ravages of the weekend flying and in the evening lecturing to auxiliary Waafs and airmen on service training. Tuesdays and Wednesdays we got into mischief wherever we could and Thursdays and Fridays were spent servicing and preparations for the weekend flying programme. Sunday was the occasion when some of the Pilots brought along their assorted girlfriends and families, and it was then that we took on the status of a flying club. Our regular RAF Adjutant was a F/O Gundry-White who also fulfilled the role of flying instructor and I think our auxiliary pilots under training (which was most of them at the time) would phone up and make arrangements to do a spot of flying. I remember very well my first week when several of the pilots came to the airfield to do just that: one of them landed in a potato field and damaged one of our Tutor aircraft, another

one force-landed in a field and ran into a hedge with a
Tiger Moth, and a third one damaged our other Moth
when he landed by mistake at Biggin Hill! Now I was
familiar by this time with the Squadron Motto (*Conjunctis
Viribus*) but in view of the past week's capers by our pilots I
was beginning to wonder if we should not now make a
substitution and use instead the opening words of Psalm
483 ancient and modern (*We Plough The Fields And Scat-
ter*).

Night flying at Kenley was particularly hazardous. The
runway lighting was the same as that used on Flying Training Schools, 'Goose Neck' flares and a 'Chance Light', the
latter being a very powerful searchlight mounted on a
mobile platform and stationed at the approach end of the
landing strip. It was used mainly as a last resort to show up
the landing strip if a pilot was unsure of himself, but it also
had the same effect on anybody who happened to be on the
flare path as the headlights of a car have on a rabbit and I
can assure you that it was no use singing 'Run Rabbit Run'
when an incoming aircraft was bearing down on you! We
always had a substantial number of Auxiliary ground staff
who volunteered to help out on the flare path and looking
back now I wonder why it was always an Auxiliary who was
put in charge of the 'box of matches' (see Chapter 9)!

One of the regular airmen on the squadron at the time
was a Corporal George Nunn, with whom I became
friendly and who operated a modest little sideline of selling
'goodies' on credit. All permanent staff lived in one large
barrack block which comprised four separate rooms, two up
and two down, each accommodating 30 airmen. In each

room George would leave on a locker a small attaché case and a small notebook in which you would enter what you had taken from the case. The case would contain chocolate bars, packs of cigarettes, matches and those things you would normally get from the Barber – and I do not mean a haircut – known in those days as a 'packet of three' and now supplied free of charge on the NHS! George also had two toolboxes in the hangar, one, of course, packed with goodies and with the accompanying notebook. The procedure was that on Friday after pay (we were paid weekly in those days) George would come to each block and collect whatever we all owed him.

I must have been at Kenley for about 6 months when George Nunn was promoted to Sergeant. When he came and told me, and as one entrepreneur to another, he asked if I would like to carry on his 'enterprise', as he felt that now he was a Sergeant it would be unwise to continue. Naturally, I asked whether he was doing anything illegal and he said he thought not. He felt he was not a threat to the NAAFI and that provided I did not go public and start giving out share options to all and sundry, no one would worry too much. There were, however, members of the top brass who, apart from having shares in the NAAFI, might feel that Air Force rules and regulations did not allow for such an enterprise but I would not have so much to lose as he should I be 'tumbled'.

After due consideration I took on this project; George introduced me to the wholesaler who supplied him and quite successful it proved to be. I did not go out and buy a BMW straight away and unfortunately, before I was able to do so, I had to go into liquidation because the war loomed. That ******* Adolf had scored his first victory!

An interesting aspect to this venture was that during the whole of the nine months I was 'in business' I cannot recall that I lost as much as a penny or even a box of matches. Remembering how little we were all paid in those days, nobody cheated deliberately and everyone 'played the game'. I don't think that such a venture could operate today; a sad reflection on today's standards.

Life on the squadron was fairly uneventful, but I do remember one occasion when in common with most other RAF stations we had an open day. This followed the usual pattern, static exhibitions in the hangers and of course a flying display. We had, in those days, a grass covered airfield, there were no runways, and a rope kept the crowd away from the flying area. The Commanding Officer of 615 was one Squadron Leader A.V. Harvey, who, although not exactly beloved by many on the squadron was ex-RFC and an exceptional pilot. During the afternoon and whilst the flying display was going on, somehow a very drunken person had got into the airfield area and was making a general nuisance of himself. He had been quite aggressive to one or two people, the service police had been called and were trying hard to catch him.

Just at that moment one of the pilots who had been giving a display with one of our tutor aircraft landed the plane, taxied half way back to the take off end, turned the plane around, and started to get out. At this point the drunk pushed through the crowd, ducked under the rope and raced out to this aircraft. He pushed the pilot to the ground, jumped into the cockpit as the plane started to move forward and crazily moved off. Everyone was, of course, shattered at seeing the drunk flying off with this plane but worse was yet to come. He came back across the airfield at 'zero feet', pitching and tossing all over the place and then soared up into the air, turning on his back and doing the most crazy things. The spectators watching the display really had their money's worth that day! This drunk really put on a wonderful flying display and it was not until he finally landed in a most hair-raising manner and the service police had raced out to apprehend him that it was discovered that the 'drunk' was a very sober Squadron Leader Harvey and that it had all been a gimmick for the entertainment of the crowd. Not a view shared by everyone who was there!

To end this chapter I must mention the squadron's summer camp. In the summer of 1939 we went to Ford aerodrome in Sussex, which has since been turned into an open prison, so it is possible that many of you have returned to this place! We all settled in for what we hoped would be an enjoyable couple of weeks. The squadron comprised of two flights, 'A' and 'C'. A Flight's colour was blue, C Flight's colour was yellow (or perhaps the other way round...) Anyway, C Flight acquired a billy-goat as their mascot and painted its horns and hooves bright yellow. Not to be outdone and being in A Flight, on the way to Littlehampton on our first night out I bought from a petrol station, for the sum of 2/6d, a white duck (they didn't have a blue one) and managed to obtain some wide blue ribbon which was tied around Donald's neck. We had an interesting evening but we did discover that ducks are not really 'cuddly' pets; they have a habit of leaving 'trademarks' liberally everywhere – embarrassing. On our way home, now sometime around midnight, we came across a boating lake at Littlehampton amusement park, and of course the unanimous suggestion was to let Donald have a swim. I lowered him (or her) into the water and with a shake of the head the ribbon came adrift and the duck was free. We spent the next half hour trying to retrieve the thing, all getting soaked up to our waists (though, needless to say, we were all well 'soaked' before we got anywhere near the lake). Eventually we did catch the duck, secured him with the ribbon, the colour of which had now run, and – bingo – we had a blue duck!

And then, not entirely to everyone's surprise, came our recall to Kenley. Hitler was on the move and the balloon was about to go up. World War II was about to start...

12. Croydon Capers

We returned to Kenley from our aborted summer camp at Ford aerodrome not knowing just what was in store for all of us, quickly discovering, however, that there were lots of things about to happen. My own personal problem was what I was to do with Donald, the squadron mascot! I had quickly realised that an operational airfield was no place to keep pets but as we had moved so quickly from Ford, I had not been able to find a home for him at such short notice. I made a few enquiries on the station and was sent along to see a lady who lived nearby, whom, I was told, would probably like to have our duck. By a strange coincidence, the lady's name was Drake and when I told her about Donald she said she would love to have him. Little did I realise that her interpretation of the word 'have' was not the same as mine. When I saw this same lady coming out of the local grocer's store clutching a large bag of green peas I surmised that 'Donald' was indeed being 'had'!

We were kept very busy, being involved in an intense flying programme, getting our pilots up to what was considered 'operational standard'. We also had an 'Embodiment Ceremony' at which all our Auxiliary personnel were to become an integral part of the RAF which would make us all one large, happy family. As was the custom with families at that time, 'leftover' elderly members would be placed in the care of their unfortunate juniors – and this is what happened to us with regard to our aircraft! At that time we had a few medium-aged Gladiators and a few very old Gauntlets and these were passed over to a training unit for 'demolition exercises' whilst in return we received replacement Gladiators from 605 County of Warwick Squadron, who in turn were to be re-equipped with Hurricane Mark Is (the lucky b*****s!).

Being mainly an auxiliary station, Kenley had been a very free and easy station with lots of privileges, but the crisis quickly changed all that and in no time at all there were suddenly more 'brown types' on the station than airmen, discipline and security were rigorously enforced and we were challenged wherever we went. For the first time the word 'Stalag' reared its ugly head! Happily this situation did not last long, for on September 2nd the squadron was posted just down the road to Croydon airport, which had now been decreed an RAF station. From there we would now defend London in its hour of need.

Our aircraft were dispersed on the west side of the airport at the rear of the houses which lined Foresters Drive and accommodation for the ground staff was to be the old Imperial Airways workshops. Our beds comprised three narrow planks of wood which rested on a pair of trestles which kept our bodies just three inches off the concrete ground! We were also each given a 'palliasse' which we stuffed with straw and which was to be our mattress, one blanket and a bolster also filled with straw ensured that we slept as snug as a 'bug in a rug'; the only thing missing was the 'Keatings'!

We had almost completed 'picketing' our aircraft to the ground (this was before the days to come of readiness and scrambles) when a faint murmuring was heard and which became louder by the second and then suddenly across the airfield, in formation, came the aircraft of No.17 Squadron who, together with No.3 Squadron, were to share the airfield with us. The sound of nineteen Hurricanes with their Merlin engines was to me one of the most thrilling thing I had ever heard and even to this day the individual sound of a Merlin engine is music to my ears – a sound I will never forget (some folk, I know, will call it a 'noise', but this I will never accept, although I will agree that it some-times 'growled', but lots of thoroughbreds will do just this!)

You will, I am sure, forgive me if I digress a little and say just a few more words about the fabulous Merlin engine and what a wonderful piece of machinery it was. It was indeed the ultimate in piston engine design, the best and most powerful ever built, with very few vices and a joy to work on; and of course, it marked the 'end of an era' for this type of aircraft power plant. In retrospect it also marked the end of an era for the type of aircraft we were involved in at that time. The Hawker Fury, Gauntlet, Gladiator, Hurri-cane and Supermarine Spitfire were all single-seater fighters each powered by Bristol or Rolls engine and they seemed to me to be graceful, almost gentle aircraft which did a wonderful job in a relatively quiet and efficient man-ner. It was a different story when the 'jets' arrived – these were real 'killer' aircraft which certainly let one know when they were about and it always felt to me as if they were trying to beat one into the ground with their noise – no 'purring' was ever to be heard from them!

As previously mentioned, our aircraft dispersal point was at the end of the gardens of the houses along Forester's Drive, which were separated by six foot iron railings from the aerodrome itself. Most of the houses had been evacuated by their owners but we were fortunate in having one of our machines positioned immediately at the rear of two houses which were still occupied. In one of these lived a Mr Montague Bridges with his wife and their two children, Jack and Jill, with whom we very soon became friendly. Within an hour of our arrival Mrs Bridges was at the railings with a large tray on which were pots of tea and heaps of cakes, hungry airmen for the use of, and weren't they appreciated? This was a pattern that was followed by all the family during the two months we were stationed there, they were so kind to all of us. Of course, in no time at all we had cut through the railings and were invited into the house to partake of meals, play cards and listen to Mrs Bridges play the piano, which she did very well.

The following day, September 3rd, was a day we all remember. I and several of the lads of the squadron were having our elevenses in the NAAFI, which had been set up in the old Control Building, when we heard on the radio that we were at war with Germany. It was an awful moment, the atmosphere most strange. A few remarks were made that were meant to be funny, but fun was somehow not on the menu that day and no one laughed. We had all been expecting this to happen, but now that it had come we were all at a loss to know what to do. The future seemed very uncertain. Little did any of us know that life for everybody would never be the same again, that laughs would be few and far between and that this conflict would last such a long time and cost so many lives.

We were still talking amongst ourselves and discussing this news when the air raid siren went off and this created something of a panic, as no one knew what to do.

"What the hell…' said one 'bod'.

"Sounds like the Wall's man," said another. "Anyone for an ice lolly?"

Then our Flight Commander, a certain Tommy Thornley, poked his head around the door and shouted 'Get to your aircraft as fast as you can, we are being attacked!'

We just dropped everything, left the building and dashed across to our aircraft, which were at the opposite side of the airfield – and didn't the 'Woodbines' take their toll? When we reached our dispersal we found pilots in all the aircraft and a couple had started up, but they were not sure what to do next. Squadron Leader Harvey was running up and down in front of the machines with a revolver in his hand, steel helmet on and gas mask slung, like everyone else, awaiting orders. At this point we were 'saved by the bell' or rather by the 'all clear'; everyone heaved a sigh of relief and wondered what had been learned by the exercise, if anything at all.

Being so close to the town of Croydon with all the amenities it had to offer combined with the care and consideration we received from Mrs Bridges, her family and friends made our life very pleasant during our stay at Croydon. I was also very fortunate that my home in London was nearby and it was most convenient to be able pop home when leave allowed. I had two old school friends still living in the area whom I would see on my visits home. They were courting two sisters and when I was informed that the squadron was to be sent over to France within a week I managed to get a couple of days off, went to London, met up with my friends and also met a *third* sister. She is still with me today (more about this anon).

And so on November 15th 1939 I left Croydon for Merville in France aboard an Armstrong Whitworth Ensign, filled with apprehension, and landed to find myself up to my knees in mud with no sign of any 'entente cordiale' in evidence...

13.   The Lull Before...

Merville, France, November 1939 – cold, raining, windy and mud up to our knees; moreover, our French allies did not appear to be overly enthusiastic in their welcome to us. Our first duty was to get our aircraft refuelled and here we made our first acquaintance with the ubiquitous 'four gallon petrol container' and the chamois leather with which all refuelling would be done for the next few months. How we came to hate this task! I wonder what happened to all those thousands of empty containers we left behind – turned into Dornier bombers, I suppose!

My number one priority was to sort out some kind of accommodation for all the ground staff and I went with our flight commander, F/Lt Tommy Thornley, into Merville town to look at an old grain silo which had been allocated for our use as living accommodation. We eventually found a very dilapidated old building and I was somewhat surprised when Mr Thornley remarked that he thought it looked most interesting and that it could be very accommodating! With some misgivings on my part I felt it was opportune to inform him that that was exactly the same remark made by some of the early Christians when they first saw the Coliseum in Rome, and we all know what happened on that occasion! However, with no other option we had to accept what was on offer and subsequently moved in. That night, however, I had reasons to once again give a little thought to the goings on within the Coliseum. You see, the existing residents of our new habitat, whom we thought had moved on, did their level best to eat us alive as we tried to sleep. I refer of course to the local 'rats', who I think wanted us to move out. Resourceful as ever, we all found ways of elevating our beds and belongings well above the concrete floor and the rats did not fare so well on the second night and eventually moved on to a new eating place. This period of the war was boring, miserable and uncomfortable for mostly everyone, neither side made any moves as far as hostilities were concerned. Although we heard that the RAF were being concerned!

It did take the form of a propaganda operation involving the dropping of leaflets (German bums for the use of) and which was known by the aircrew who did the delivery as the toilet paper run, it did, however, keep the dust from settling on the few bombers we had at that time.

Our Squadron spent the early days at Merville carrying out sector patrols about the area to familiarise themselves with local and it was on one of these sorties that we sustained our first fatality of the war. A number of our auxiliary pilots were not quite up to operational standard at the outbreak of the war and we had posted to us several fully experienced pilots from other squadrons. One of these was a Flying Officer Wickham, who came to us from No.3 Squadron. It was during one of these sector patrols that for some reason never discovered he crashed his Gladiator in a potato field, completely destroying it and leaving wreckage everywhere, further endorsing my recommendation regarding the Squadron motto. I , together with a 3-ton Leyland, a driver and one Bill Blunt were sent off to bring back the remains of the pilot, a most unpleasant task.

For the next six months we experienced what came to be called the 'Phoney War', because just nothing happened except that the weather became wetter and much colder and we were so unprepared. We did very little flying as our aircraft were mostly frozen into the mud and immovable, we certainly could not have 'scrambled', (a word that came into its own at a later date). The Pegasus engines of our aircraft had to be kept warm nevertheless and as the 'night lights' placed under each engine was not quite up to this task we had to start and run up the engines frequently. Aircraft of that era were at a sloping angle with tail wheel on the ground when parked and in a very short time because oil was not getting up to the airscrew reduction unit in sufficient amounts they all seized up.

Christmas was now getting very near and we heard rumours that leave for some of us was being considered, my two friends in London had informed me that they had decided to marry the sisters (see Chapter 12) in a Double Wedding at Christmas and if I could get home we would make it a 'triple' effort! Unfortunately, this was not to be. I did not get my leave until February, my leave boat being escorted by three destroyers. Someone was making very sure I did not duck the issue this time! Married we were, and I am proud and happy to state that after 62 years we are still together.

This was to be a very happy few days and I took this opportunity to pay a visit to Mr and Mrs Bridges and their family with my new bride to express the thanks for myself and my other Squadron friends for all the kindness they had given to all of us whilst we were at Croydon and for all the goodies sent to us in France.

And it is with much sadness that I write this paragraph, a sadness which is still with me whenever I think back to this awful event. I went back from my few days leave on February 19th 1940 and had only been back a short while when I received the devastating news that Mrs Bridges and her daughter Jill had been killed by an aeroplane crash on Croydon Airfield. When we received further details of this awful event, it was revealed that a trainee pilot of 92 Squadron was sent off on his first solo in his Blenheim and it was late evening and getting dark. He failed to get height and crashed into the roof at the back of the Bridges house (which, as I explained previously, backed onto the aerodrome itself) rupturing the petrol tanks and pouring flaming petrol down the back of the house.

Witnesses stated that Mrs Bridges ran out from the back of the house holding her daughter in her arms and they were both immediately engulfed in flames. Mr Bridges ran out with Jack, his son, and although suffering some burns these did not prove fatal. A young guardsman on duty nearby took the little girl from her mother, tore off her clothing which was on fire and took her to the nearby guardroom. Another soldier covered Mrs Bridges (who by this time had her clothing burnt off her and was naked) with an overcoat and took her into a nearby house. The whole family was taken to Carshalton Hospital where sadly, but mercifully, Mrs Bridges and her small daughter died the next morning, Sunday February 25th. A full account of this tragic accident is related in more detail in a booklet by Douglas Cluett entitled 'Croydon Airport and the Battle for Britain', a book of great interest and well worth reading. In retrospect, had the family run from the house from the front and not the back, they could all have probably escaped, and how very sad that a family who had been so kind and caring for us in the RAF should be destroyed by us. After by return from Dunkirk I immediately tried to get in touch with Mr Bridges. The fire brigade in Croydon told me he had gone to stay with relatives at Herne Hill just outside of London.

I made some enquiries to the local police and although they were aware of the sad event and knew where Mr Bridges was living they declined to give the address and suggested that, for the time being, I should give up my search and hinted that Mr Bridges was feeling very bitter about things, something I could well understand, and here a chapter ends.

14.   A French Farce

The situation in France was still, as the 'natives' would have it, "drole de guerre" – and very queer it was indeed. The weather had improved but still nothing had happened and everyone was fed up to the teeth. We had moved from Merville and had stayed at several different airfields before finally settling at Abbeville. Our accommodation here was the best to date. We were billeted in very comfortable huts scattered in some woods adjacent to the airfield and here we received the good news that we were to be re-equipped with Hurricane Mk I aircraft, which lifted the spirits of everyone. It not only gave our pilots the opportunity to get in plenty of flying hours to familiarise themselves with their new aircraft, but also allowed we ground staff to learn as much as we could about these planes. With this in mind, 'the powers that be' decided to send my flight to a place called Le Touquet, a delightful seaside resort on the coast. This was an event we all looked forward to, but which, unfortunately, was to be very short lived. We moved into Le Touquet on May 9th to be accommodated in huts on the perimeter of the airfield and our pilots to stay in very 'up-market' hotels in the town. As we all now know, the very next day, May 10th, Herr Hitler decided to make his move and 'the balloon went up' with a vengeance. We on the airfield were awakened at dawn by the sound of low-flying aircraft and some very unhealthy sounding bangs! A few of the 'brighter sparks' in the hut were up and getting dressed and quickly ran out to see what was going on, immediately informing all and sundry that we were being attacked. Within seconds we were all out of the hut and watching the air display! Our beautiful Hurricanes, which we had meticulously lined up in review order, wing tip to wing tip, were now burning merrily and a pair of enemy aircraft were leisurely flying up and down the row at about 50 feet and machine gunning what was left. They then turned their attention to 'the spectators' and proceeded to plaster us with what they had left in their armoury before flying home for a belated breakfast. Fortunately, nobody was even injured but we all had the fear of Christ put into us.

We felt at this point that it was safe to assume the war had started in earnest, that our services may be required and that we ought to return to Abbeville, if only to collect some more aircraft; we certainly could not do very much with what we had left.

And so we returned to our base. As we were driving through the town of Abbeville we were showered with gifts by the local French inhabitants – these 'gifts' being anything that was bad or rotten in the way of meat, fish or veg. Apparently what had upset our allies was that the Luftwaffe had not only bombed Le Touquet but also had attacked every location where British forces were installed, including the town of Abbeville itself, which had been quite heavily bombed, hitting several houses and killing people.

As far as I was concerned, the next three weeks were a nightmare. Nobody seemed to know just what was happening: communications had really broken down, we had

Blenheim bombers landing, re-fuelling and taking off for goodness knows where, several Lysanders dropped in and then flew off, our own aircraft were scattered all over northern France, various 'bods' of many ranks came and went and for some reason I was reminded of the phrase 'headless chickens'. You can well imagine our reactions when an order came from someone (who shall remain nameless, only because nobody had a clue as to who it could have been ... possibly Goebbels?) telling us to get out as fast as we could. By 'out' we assumed they meant France, which we all thought an excellent idea and we promptly set about fulfilling the order in all haste. And so I found myself in the driving cab of a Leyland truck with a driver and one of my fitters, a chap named Arthur Holmes, with an assortment of 'bods' in the back. (Is there anyone still around who remembers this?).

We arrived on the outskirts of Amiens to be confronted by a couple of military redcaps who told us we were going in the wrong direction and that unless we wished to join the German troops we should turn around and go back the way we had come. Apparently, some German motorcyclists were already in the town centre. We promptly about-faced and as it had been suggested that we might get on a boat leaving Boulogne, this is where we made for. Our journey was uneventful except for a little air activity, which prompted the topical question 'theirs' or 'ours' – the knowing ones in the back providing the answers (made, of course, with fingers tightly crossed). It was almost dusk when we reached the outskirts of Boulogne and as we approached the dock area we were once again met by army

MPs who informed us that nothing would be leaving until the next day and that we should follow a service jeep which would take us to a dispersal point out of the town. This we did. They led us to a place hidden in forestry and overlooking the harbour. Several other vehicles of the squadron were also there and we settled down for the night, having been told that we would be collected in the morning. None of us had eaten much since that morning; we had stopped at a café on the way from Amiens but all we were able to get was some fluid called 'soup' and a solid called 'bread' plus whatever in the way of victuals we had secreted about our person.

A few of the lads went foraging, but most of us just wanted to get out heads down and hoped the morning would come soon so that we really could get home. The Luftwaffe, however, had their own ideas about that for they hammered Boulogne Docks all night and we had a ringside seat – and most impressive it certainly was – the whole area becoming, it seemed, one huge fire. The raid eased off just before dawn and I did manage to get a little sleep but awoke feeling cold and very hungry and decided to go and see if I could find a café open. I remembered that on our way the previous night we had passed what had looked like shops and, so, taking my greatcoat I set off to see what I could find. After a short while I entered a street, which led out of the forest and almost immediately I was aware of a wonderful smell of freshly baked bread, but could see no sign of a shop! A little further on and still following the smell I suddenly found the source, a private house; the front room had been converted into a kind of shop and the baking was all being done in the basement – and of course they were shut! However, I could see people working at making bread so I went up to the door and rang the bell. A very pleasant lady opened the door, looked at me with a very puzzled expression and asked me, in English, what I required. I very briefly explained who I was and why I was calling at her house and at that moment a man appeared at her side and took over, he too speaking in English, but with an accent I had heard before. He also wanted to know who I was. After explaining my situation he asked me in and took me into what was obviously their dining/sitting room, where he told me his name was John Edwards, a Welshman born in Swansea. He had returned to France after the Great War, married the French lady I had first spoken to and had set up as a baker, which was his trade before he had been called up. We had quite a chat about what had and what was now happening and he insisted that I stay and have some breakfast. And what a breakfast they gave me! It must be the best breakfast I have ever eaten. He returned to the kitchen to finish his baking and I, having finished my food, took my coffee, sat in a more comfortable chair, and promptly fell asleep! It was after 12 noon when my host, who had very kindly allowed me to sleep, realising I was in need of the rest, awakened me. I told them I must dash off immediately. They would not let me go, however, until they had prepared a parcel of goodies for me to take back to the other lads, for which I thanked them profusely before I bade them goodbye. I have often wondered what happened to those kind people.

Eventually I found my way back to where the lorry had been parked, but it was no longer there and the whole area was deserted. I would have to make my own way down to the harbour, which was still burning.

I reached the harbour at about 4.30 in the afternoon and was promptly taken into custody by the military police, who were not happy with my explanation as to who I was. I was taken in front of an interrogating officer and because I had no documents of any description, I was eyed very suspiciously. Another officer was called and again I had to go over my story, but he did ask me if I was wearing identity discs, something I had completely forgotten, but which I was wearing. Now, I am sure most of you will remember 'dog tags' – one was red and the other green and each was embossed with your service and service number. The red one indicated whether you were sufficiently "browned" on each side, should you get yourself involved in a fire, it was fireproof; the green one was the one the fishes spit out after they had eaten you.

They did, however, come to my rescue and I was released, but not before they had told me that no further transport would be leaving from Boulogne and that I should make my way to Calais if I had any ideas of getting back to England. Things were somewhat chaotic on the dockside and so I considered it inopportune to ask either of these officers at what time the next bus left for Calais! I did not have to worry too much, all kinds of transport were on the move and they were all going one way, my way. I managed to get on a lorry that was filled with soldiers from a guards regiment and off we went, everybody commenting on what a b****** shambles it all was and wondering what the outcome of all this was to be. We had barely moved out of Boulogne when enemy aircraft shot us up. We all left the lorry and dived into anything that could give us cover, realising that we truly were in the war for real. We got back on our lorry and set off again. There was no longer a question of 'theirs or ours' they were all 'theirs' and we did wonder where the hell the RAF were – and guess who got most of the stick – as though they all belonged to me! We reached Calais without further mishap, only to be told by more service police to 'stay on our bikes' (as one wag put it) and make our way to a place called Dunkirk, where luxury liners were waiting to take us home…

Dunkirk was about 30 miles further north and enemy action appeared to be increasing. We had already had to vacate our truck several times on the journey from Calais and I was convinced now that the Luftwaffe were looking for me personally; the thought of further travel into the unknown was a little upsetting. However, we did push on. It was getting quite dark and this we thought would make it harder for enemy aircraft to find us. We were, of course, travelling without lights, but as we seemed to be travelling in convoy, everything was on the move, all going towards Dunkirk, all we had to do was keep close to the truck in front. We were stopped by police at a place called St-Pol-sur-Mer which, we were told, was on the outskirts of Dunkirk and told to park off the road for the night and that we could go on to Dunkirk in the morning.

It was here that we had a great stroke of luck. I, together with several of the soldiers on my truck, went off to find something to eat and drink and finished up in a café facing the seafront. After tucking into a meal of omelette and chips, accompanied by several bottles of local wine, I got into conversation with a group of English fellows who had been working on a dredging machine moored by the local jetty and who told me that although they had not finished their work, the ship was seaworthy and they were going back to England with it the next day, as things were beginning to look unhealthy here. I asked if they were able to take any passengers and they told me they would take as many as wanted to go. Only a couple of the soldiers decided to come with me, the rest felt they must obey orders and we left them behind.

And that is how I got out of France. We had a good view of Dunkirk and the beach from out in the Channel; there was quite a lot of activity and quite a lot of places were burning, but the real exodus had not finally begun. That was to come within the next few days, so I was really lucky. Arriving at Dover with no identity, no money and a vague story to tell, I thought I was going to have all kinds of problems but I found everybody very helpful. I was told to go home when I said I lived in London and to telephone Kenley, my home station, and get my instructions from them. I was given a travel voucher and ten shillings as petty cash and hurriedly boarded a train for Victoria, to spend the next hour thinking of all that had happened in the past few days and wondering what next was in store for everyone...

15.   So Many: So Few

After my return from France I eventually became reunited with 615 Squadron at Kenley. We were very speedily re-equipped with replacement Hurricanes and here all credit must be given to the determination and foresight of Air Chief Marshal (Stuffy) Dowding and his staff, for ensuring that adequate fighting forces were kept at home to safe-guard any emergency – a decision which was to make certain of our salvation.

Much has been written of the events which were about to overtake us and we of 615 Squadron were to find ourselves at the centre of what became known as the Battle of Britain. My own recollection of that time was of an overwhelming sense of comradeship amongst all personnel involved including all the pilots, ground crews and ancillary staff with whom we worked. It was a period of hard work and long hours for we service personnel and for our pilots, many of whom we had become friends with, it was to be a most daunting challenge. We were to witness the transformation of carefree youths into serious adults who were ready to kill or be killed – the period has been called, and truly was "a summer for heroes".

Our airfield, of course, came under attack on several occasions and I will never forget how I hated the sound of the Tannoy: the infernal thing would say, "Air raid imminent, all personnel not servicing aircraft must take cover. Dive,

Dive, Dive!" and we were all out on the airfield like sitting ducks. Yes, this was a most 'twittering time'.

Sunday 18th August was to be our "gala day", when the Luftwaffe really tried to take us out. An attack was made at around lunchtime (perhaps they thought we would all be in the NAAFI scoffing wads and things) and was carried out by a sortie of many aircraft, both high and low flying. The low flying attack was made by a flight of nine Dornier Do17s who, it seemed, came past the guardroom at about 50 feet (but did not report in to anyone!). Four 'peeled off' and attacked the dispersal bays on our side of the airfield; the remaining five attacked the bays on the other side. Fortunately, most of our aircraft were airborne, but some work was being done on two aircraft on the airfield and I was with one of these. We had a grandstand view of the four German planes flying very low and following the perimeter track, spraying everything in sight with machine gun bullets before dropping their 'goodies' for our consumption. Sadly two of our fitters were killed in this attack and the subsequent high level attack resulted in eight further fatalities and extensive damage to the airfield, hangars and other buildings.

The battle continued on an extensive scale for almost another month and then, suddenly and overnight, the severity of the Luftwaffe's attacks came to a halt. On the morning of 16th September, we, the pilots and ground crews, arrived at our dispersal at the crack of dawn as we had done over the past months. Aircraft were brought to readiness and we who had worked throughout the night repairing and patching up planes which had been damaged were relieved to find we could muster a full flight of six planes and were ready for the fray. Pilots were strapped into their aircraft, crews stood by and starters were plugged in; apprehensively we all waited – and nothing happened! For quite a while the silence was ominous; it was quite eerie. We were taken off 'readiness' and put on 'standby' and that was how the whole day progressed. We were scrambled several times during the day but our pilots were not confronted by the very large formations encountered previously. It would be inaccurate, however, to suggest that the Luftwaffe were fighting shy. The previous day had been their most costly. We claimed to have shot down 185 of their aircraft and this had obviously had an effect on the thinking of the German High Command.

Although the battle continued on what appeared to be not quite so vicious a scale, it was still very demanding on our aircrews, who by now were feeling the strain of the constant pressure put upon them. It was also having its effect on the enemy; during the month of October, the Luftwaffe lost 325 planes. We had our losses too; Fighter Command had almost 100 pilots killed and almost as many injured. This attrition just could not continue and although spasmodic attacks continued for quite a while, this phase of the Battle for Britain came to an end.

The Luftwaffe then changed their tactics and opted for an all-out night-time attack on England, with the most devastating and terrifying effect.

When that phase of the battle, which mainly involved Fighter Command, was more or less over, the Air Ministry claimed that between July 10th and October 31st a total of

2,698 German aircraft had been destroyed (however, later records show that the actual figure was 1,733). The German High Command's claims were even more optimistic; they claimed they had destroyed 3,058 British fighters. In fact, the RAF lost 915 aircraft. The toll in aircrew was also extremely high. In total the RAF lost 415 pilots, but it is interesting to note that some 451 pilots successfully went unscathed through the whole battle.

It had been a most trying and demanding period for everyone involved and despite all the training we had been given up to that time we were hardly equipped for what we were faced with. This particularly applied to our pilots, who had to learn new methods and ways of combat to survive – and how well they coped. It really was the proving time for the RAF and this was when it came of age.

I regret and apologise to you all that this episode of my memoirs has been lacking in the type of humour that I have tried to impart in previous efforts, but I am sure you will all appreciate that there were not many occasions for frivolity. Living at the time was much too serious and hardly a day passed when we were not aware that someone we had worked with, or even a close friend, would not be around any more.

I am very proud that I took part in this battle and I feel sure that I speak for many old lads still kicking around when I say that it was an honour and a privilege to have served alongside just some of "The Few".

16. We Take the High Road

As far as 615 Squadron was concerned, the Battle of Britain was over and, like all the other squadrons who had taken part, we were feeling a trifle weary and so it was decided that we should be 'put out to graze'. Little did we know that for the next 18 months we were to embark on a real 'Cook's Tour'.

It may be of interest at this point to explain how all the movements came about. The Air Ministry had a department known as 'Records', which also had an integral section that dealt with 'Movements'. No, I am not referring to any bodily functions which may come to mind, this section of the RAF is responsible for the posting and transference of men and machines ... to the wrong places at the wrong time. Did you know that an overseas troopship, usually HMS *Somerset*, sailed from Liverpool dock fully loaded with servicemen every year on Christmas Eve? Thankfully, the war put a stop to this nonsense. Where could they send us to anyway? One other odd thing about this department is that no one ever seemed to meet anyone who worked there or knew where they operated. The result was that a lot of speculation arose about these people. It was hinted that they could be of a religious order – they certainly 'moved in mysterious ways, their blunders to perform'. I have heard them described as little men with very large heads out of which protruded antenna-like probes that allowed them to interfere with the lives of all airmen. If the stories are to be believed, they also had huge bulbous eyes (blinkered, of course). But these people were all powerful; they controlled where you lived, how you lived and even if you lived. In the early days I heard them referred to as 'boffins', but they scarcely lived up to that one. Their cousins were, of course, more familiar on the flights and throughout the squadron – I refer to those playful little pranksters we all knew as 'gremlins'. One of their favourite pranks was to perch on the shoulder of a pilot and just as he was about to touch down they would raise his undercarriage. Great fun that! They would nudge the arm of a fitter just as he had finally positioned a nut onto an inaccessible bolt down in the bowels of an engine and it was one of these jokers who would make certain that the slice of bread you had just buttered would fall out of your hand onto the floor – butter side down.

And so, with all these 'friends' trying to help, we found ourselves posted as a squadron to an airfield in Scotland called Prestwick, where we hoped we would stay quite a while, away from all the action. Six weeks later we were on our way back again. The reason for this was to do with our Scottish uniform – the 'sporran' was not conducive to good flying order, it would keep getting caught around the 'joy stick'. Back to London we came and were stationed at Northolt, living and working with our Polish Allies, who had two squadrons of fighters on the station at that time. My outstanding memory of this posting was to witness what I considered an extremely brave operation on the part of four Polish Aircrew. We were ordered to prepare, for a secret flight, two Fairey Battle aircraft that had been flown in especially for this operation. Two Polish Pilots and their navigators were to attack a specified target deep inside German territory and everyone was aware that these aircraft could not possibly carry enough fuel for a return flight. It was, therefore, a 'one-way ticket' for the aircrews. When they were about to take off, the crews handed over all their personal belongings; photos, badges, watches, rings, etc, to all the friends they were leaving behind and with smiles and waves they taxied out on the runway. We were all aware of the kind of reception they would receive, as Polish Nationals, should the Germans capture them; brave men indeed.

We heard nothing more about these Poles, as once again we were moved on, this time being sent back to our old base at Kenley. We were happy to be going home, particularly as we hoped to be there in time for Christmas. We were to stay at Kenley for the next four months and whilst we were all happy to be on our home base – the majority of our personnel lived nearby – the German High Command were stepping up the nightly 'blitz' on targets in Great Britain and at that moment were mainly attacking London and the surrounding area. It was, indeed, a most harrowing and worrying period, for each night we on the airfield could see London and all around going up in flames, knowing that our families were somewhere in the midst of it all. We were, of course, able to get home and visit relatives quite frequently and although this was indeed a bonus, I have to admit that whilst it was sad to say our farewells and return to camp, I always felt much safer there than staying in London. I did, indeed, pity the unfortunate civilians having to just grin and bear it all.

It was, however, with some misgivings that we received the news that 'Movements' had decided we should have another 'holiday'; this was at the end of April 1941 – but where to send us? The Germans had their towels on all the deckchairs at all the resorts in France. 'Monty' had his hands full with unwelcome and unruly visitors in the Mediterranean and the only 'package tour' on offer was going to the Far East, but none of us was very keen on Chinese wedding cake, so that was out. We were eventually sent off to a place called Valley, located on the Isle of Anglesey, North Wales. There we found lots of sand and sand dunes, but the wind was blowing like the clappers and the natives were not very friendly. The best they could do, I suppose!

With Anglesey being very near Liverpool, our main port for the entry of all the country's needs, we were ordered, as a squadron, to carry out patrols over the area, as ships were constantly being attacked by the Luftwaffe, many being sunk. We stayed at Valley throughout the summer, almost four months, and most enjoyable it was. I managed to get a very healthy tan and make a few friends amongst the locals (the only way to get a drink on a Sunday). I don't think we shot down many of the enemy, in fact shipping losses went up, so at that point it was decided we should move off (whilst we still had some ships left!) and so we changed resorts.

We left Valley and moved down to Manston, on the Kentish coast, where we could keep a wary eye on enemy action in the English Channel. Our aircraft carried out sweeps across the coast of France, attacked enemy shipping and hostile aircraft – but all at a price. We lost several of our pilots. It was a very busy period for everyone and after a couple of months it was accepted that we had all had enough and that it was time to move on again.

This time, once again, we were packed off to Wales, the remotest part, a place called Angle, situated on the extreme toe of the Welsh peninsula, jutting out into the Irish Sea. It was very desolate, bleak, extremely windy and rained most of the time. To all of us it was the end of the world. Our pilot's duties were again to carry out protective patrols above tankers bringing in much-needed oil to the nearby port of Milford Haven. With the exception of the lucky ones that went on leave, we all remained and had to spend our Christmas here – and a miserable time was had by all.

My sole memory of this posting was that I almost became a casualty of this war. It came about this way. In my flight at this time there were four Norwegian pilots attached to us, excellent chaps and very friendly. We, the Flight, were accommodated in two Nissen-type buildings, one for the ground staff, with all of their tools etc, and the other for the pilots. I had, at this point, been promoted to Flight Sergeant in charge of our flight and the only space available for my office table was in the same 'hut' as the pilots, but at the far corner and near the only window. One morning I was sitting at this table doing some flight work or other when there was an almighty 'bang'. Dust fell down from the roof and daylight appeared where it should not have done. About six inches above my left ear there was quite a large hole which the breeze came wafting through. It transpired that one of our Norwegian pilots had been cleaning his revolver, had not unloaded it, and one was 'up the spout'. It was what one would call a 'near miss'. He was, of course, very apologetic and insisted that I must put him on a charge, which of course I just would not do. I was very pleased to forget all about the incident, particularly when I realised what might have happened. I have had a 'twitch' on that side ever since.

I was to take part in one more posting with the squadron and this was to another airfield in Wales, this time to a place called Fairwood Common. I did not know at the time but this was to see the parting of the way for 615 Squadron and me. We had been informed that we were to be part of a three squadron wing and that we were to be sent to the Far East. What really transpired will all be revealed in the next chapter. Finally I think that 'Records' and 'Movements' had lived up to their reputations and had given us a fair run around. They do say 'you can't win 'em all'!

17. RAF Gatwick 1942

Still at Fairwood Common and awaiting the inevitable posting to I knew not where, being as usual at the mercy of our old friends 'Records', I was surprised to be summoned to the squadron office to see our CO. At this meeting he confirmed that, although I would be leaving the squadron, I would be joining a squadron that was to be part of the wing being sent out to the Far East and that we would therefore all still be working together, which softened the blow of parting from 615 somewhat.

I was to be posted to No 239 Squadron, an army co-operation outfit which at that time was flying American Tomahawk aircraft fitted with Allison engines but was to be re-equipped with Hurricanes for the sortie out east, where my experience with this aircraft would be required.

On 16th February 1942 I said my farewells to all my 615 colleagues, temporarily I hoped, and took myself off to RAF Gatwick, as it was then known, where my new squadron was stationed. Gatwick was then a small grass-covered airfield, used mainly by local flying clubs and a few small commercial aircraft companies, mainly handling freight but with the odd passenger or two. The airfield did, however, have two outstanding features, one being the well known 'Beehive', a low, two-storey, completely circular structure, which housed all the requirements to operate an airfield; customs, reception areas, catering facilities, general stores and various other offices. It was a very busy complex indeed, truly a 'beehive' in every way, and when we arrived things really started to 'buzz'.

The other unique feature was that the airfield had its own small 'sewage farm' to cater for the requirements of the small number of personnel using the airfield at that time. This 'enterprise' was in the most capable hands of one who would be known as 'Sam' and what other possible name could there be for such a one. Truly, here was a man who in every way 'threw himself into his work' – as his presence and appearance indicated. He would often enthuse about his work and took great pride in plunging his hand in to a great pile of the 'finished product', thrusting it under one's nose and telling one to 'put that on your rhubarb and you will have the largest and finest crop in the country'. He looked a bit crestfallen when I remarked that I preferred custard on my rhubarb. He was a happy soul, however, things had been very quiet for him since the war started but our arrival had in a way added to his stock in trade and he was very grateful to welcome us.

Of course, Gatwick has, like everything else, moved on since those days. It has become much larger and many great changes have taken place. Had they not done so, should you today wish to travel from, say, Gatwick to Manchester, instead of being asked to present yourself at the airport two hours before take off you would be asked to make that two years! As for the other 'feature', had that not 'adjusted' everyone would be up to their knees in the stuff, the whole of southern England would be covered with rhubarb fields and we would be boasting to the whole world that we had the most affluent 'effluent' entrepreneur ever known. Fortunately things have moved on and we can all breathe freely.

As I mentioned earlier, the reason for my posting to this new squadron was my expertise on the Hurricane and its Rolls-Royce Merlin engine. You can therefore understand my surprise when we were duly re-equipped with American P-51s, also known as Mustangs, which were powered by Allison engines. These were good aircraft, but I like to think that because I was so upset at this switch and became 'all huffy', the Air Council, not wanting to provoke me further, decided to remove the Allison engines and replace them with Mark 20 Merlins. We now had a world-beating machine.

I was to stay at Gatwick for about nine months and although the working day was completely different from that on a fighter squadron, it was a very happy time. All personnel were billeted away from the airfield; we SNCOs all lived in what had been a private girl's school. We each had our own bedroom, a very luxurious lounge and a really super kitchen, together with the services of a first-class chef. I certainly enjoyed the best food I ever had in the service.

Nothing more had been mentioned about the Far East exercise, although I was aware that 615 had departed on their 'package tour' and were by now 'swanning around' the exotic places of the mystic east! Meanwhile, we at home were about to carry the battle to the enemy. I refer to what was a trial invasion of Europe, namely the attack on Dieppe by combined forces. As we were still an Army co-operation squadron we were involved mainly in a reconnaissance and photographic role. The cost to the squadron was two pilots and three of our Tomahawks; we also had a Boston aircraft which force landed in the garden of a house on the perimeter of our airfield. The house was owned by two very elderly folk who were very upset at unwelcome visitors who had not been invited. Two of the crew were badly injured and we had to get them into the ambulance which had arrived at the old couple's front door and this involved more aggravation with the old ones. I do not think that they were aware that there was a war going on; they appeared to be detached from it all.

The administration of the squadron was conducted from two small offices within the Beehive and one day I was summoned by our CO to present myself to Headquarters for an interview and to be wearing 'best blue'. Feeling very apprehensive, I did just that, and was introduced to a Group Captain from the Air Ministry whose name I cannot recall. He told me to take a seat and asked me to confirm that I was indeed a 'career airman' and that I was fully aware that I was subject to the 'Official Secrets Act'. You can well imagine what went through my mind. What, for goodness sake, had I done? The Tower of London appeared before me and I could visualise the executioner sharpening his axe. He then told me that I could be about to become involved in a completely new form of warfare never before practised by our armed forces and that I would have to go to 'Lashem' to fulfil this operation. Very dramatic it all sounded. I then thought about that word 'Lashem' and into my mind came a vision of 'Ben Hur', his chariots and galloping horses. Was the war going so badly for us? I wondered how long it would be before we were issued with longbows. Then I had a happy thought and my memory took me to the Westminster Embankment and a vision of Boadicea driving her chariot, pulled by three fine horses. I conjured up a vision of maybe a hundred or more bare-breasted WAAFs careering around the 'peri' track. 'That cannot be bad,' I thought, and immediately told myself to look out my farrier's manual…

The Group Captain then went on to ask me if I was familiar with the names Hengist, Horsa and Hamilcar and not wishing to be a complete idiot I said yes, I had heard of them – weren't they a Nordic variety act appearing at the London Palladium?

He looked at me oddly, as though I really was an idiot. 'No', he said, 'they are not that, they are actually the names of three types of military glider, to be used for transporting parachutists or airborne forces into battle.' He continued by telling me that the Hamilcar was the largest of these gliders, that it had been constructed to carry a 'Centurion' tank and its crew, and that a new airfield had been built to accommodate this monster at a place called Lasham, which was very close to Basingstoke. He continued to tell me that I would be required to set up workshops and that I was to order whatever I thought would be required, utilizing a war equipment schedule for a heavy bomber squadron, as we would be using Halifax aircraft for the towing of these giants. He said that nothing on this scale had ever been carried out before and that we would be working in the dark but that I would get all kinds of support.

It really did sound like a wonderful posting and a great challenge and that I was being given a choice. He told me that it was possible that at some time in the future the undertaking could involve my coming under Army discipline and Army orders and therefore I was to be given the choice of accepting or refusing. My decision was made for me when he told me that there was the possibility of an OBE in it for whoever took the job; this depending on how well they performed. (Little did I realise that his interpretation of OBE was 'Out on your Bloody Ear' and not what I took it to mean.)

So, I accepted the posting and set off for Lasham and a future that proved most interesting, although at times a little bewildering...

18. Getting Airborne

I took up my posting to Lasham during the first week of January 1943, looking forward to this new adventure with interest and expecting something special, but not knowing just what. My welcome, however, was most disappointing. With the exception of a solitary airman in the temporary guardroom, who was not interested in who I was or why I was there, there was no one about anywhere. No red carpet, not one officer of high rank and not a sign of the BBC. I am, of course, referring to the 'Bare Breasted Charioteers' (see Chapter 17), a very disappointing reception.

The station had been under construction for only a few months with just one very large hangar and several other temporary buildings for offices, messing, workshops etc. Apart from the headquarters and messing staff, there were very few people about. The CO was a Squadron Leader; a station WO and a messing officer were also there and they all lived off the station. The CO confirmed that we were to be a heavy glider training station equipped with Hamilcar tank-carrying gliders and a Halifax bomber squadron to tow these monsters. My office was a Thorne-type hut and my duties were to receive and order such goods and chattels as would be required to operate this venture and also to inter-view and employ technical staff as they arrived on site. This work had, up to this point, been carried out by a Warrant

Officer engineer who had been posted after just four weeks on the job, which made we wonder a little…

And so commenced one of the most boring and useless periods of my whole service. Nobody had a clue what was happening. In time I had posted to me some forty or more tradesmen but as we had no aircraft to work on they too soon became fed up to the teeth. Interestingly, these tradesmen were all classified as 'riggers' but were, in reality, carpenters and some were highly skilled. 'Records' must have scoured the country to find so many of them; some of them even came from abroad. I reached the point when I expected Joseph of Nazareth would turn up at any moment. The only relief I got from the boredom was when we were visited by Army personnel, who came to us quite frequently and in a variety of aircraft, which I was able to service but not able to refuel as the fuel storage area was not yet completed and no petrol was held on the base.

It was through one of these visits that I was to get a rewarding break from the tedious life I was living. I do not know what the reason was for the visits of these Army officers, all of whom bore the brevet of the Glider Pilot Regiment, but on one occasion two of them came into my office and began to ask me questions about the Hamilcar and I had to tell them that I had never seen one, in fact I had never seen any military glider at all. With that they took their leave and returned a short while later, accompanied by the CO. Apparently, they had decided it would be in the interests of all concerned if I had some idea what was going on. It was agreed that I would return with these officers to their base at a place called Tilshead in Wiltshire, not far from Devizes. So, after gathering up a few essentials I climbed aboard the Dakota in which they had arrived and returned with them.

I only stayed at Tilshead for two days but it was most instructive in many ways and I learned quite a lot in a short space of time. My first impression was that I was back on an FTS – everywhere I looked there was action and aircraft, with and without gliders, filled the whole sky. There were RAF and Army personnel everywhere and it was obvious that a very intensive flying training programme was being carried out – and most enthusiastically – by everyone. The towing aircraft were mainly Tiger Moths and Magisters with the odd Dakota. The gliders being used were Hengists, Hotspurs and Horsas and when I eventually had a closer look at them I was astonished at how flimsy and fragile they appeared considering the use for which they were intended.

I was told that a test was about to take place with one of the Horsas and would I care to go with them? I jumped at the chance. My first impression on entering the Horsa was of getting into a London Underground train. It was made to carry forty-plus airborne soldiers with all their armaments. On other occasions it could also carry a six-pounder gun, a fully laden jeep with ammunition and a crew of at least six troops. On being given this information I wondered how such a load could possibly be towed off the ground. We were to be towed off by a Dakota aircraft and although there were only about a dozen people aboard I felt a little apprehensive about the venture. But take off we did and how different it was from taking off in a powered aircraft; it was so smooth and comparatively silent with just a faint sound from the towing aircraft in front. And so, for the second time in my life, I found myself connected to my 'parent' by an 'umbilical cord' and thinking to myself that if I was to keep living this time, please don't sever it! Then suddenly, someone did just that and everything went deathly still (wrong word to use there) and we were hanging silently in space, a most peculiar sensation and a little unnerving. I had a feeling at the time that if someone, somewhere, closed a door to shut the air out, we would drop like a stone.

My concern for my wellbeing must have shown, possibly my knees knocking or my teeth chattering gave me away, but one of the troops on board told me not to fear as these gliders had been designed to land almost anywhere... (it was that word 'almost' that worried me, especially when he added 'provided no one has left a house or a haystack in the landing path!'). We did, however, land quite safely and a very enjoyable flight it had been. I could well understand the attraction for gliding as a peacetime sport, but as a wartime operation the use of gliders, I personally thought, was a little too hazardous.

I began to wonder just what type of person would volunteer for any of the airborne services, be they Glider Pilot Regiment, Air Landing Troops or Parachute Brigade, for they were all volunteers from all ranks of the British Army. From my earliest days in the RAF, I came to realise that any form of flying could be dangerous and was alien to us humans. Had we been intended to fly surely we would have been born with wings! For those of us in the RAF, however, things were helped a little, for our aircraft were provided with engines and if our pilots did get their first attempt at a landing wrong they could always abort and have another go. Not so with a glider, you were not given an option. What went up, came down, period. As regards the Glider Pilot volunteers, only men who would be able to acquire the flying skill and soldiering ability up to Battle School standard could possibly be considered. Few were accepted and fewer still finally won the coveted Blue Wings. Before he started training, before he was even considered as an applicant, his future role was made brutally clear to him. He would be required to fly a fragile wooden glider packed with heavily armed men across the sea and then to land it in the face of the most efficient, if not the finest soldiers in the world, the German Army, or die in the attempt. After landing, he would be expected to fight alongside his comrades. This is exactly what the glider pilots did, proving the truth of the regiment's motto, 'Nothing is Impossible'. But over 400 of them were killed in action.

I returned to Tilshead in a completely different frame of mind and wanting to be a part of this new type of warfare. Nothing had changed in my absence and after another couple of weeks I applied for a posting. In the course of an interview with my CO I gained the impression that he too was unhappy with the inactivity on the station and that he would certainly forward on my application.

Almost two months later my request was granted and I was informed that I was to be posted to 295 Squadron, stationed at Netheravon in Wiltshire, who were engaged on towing gliders. However, a remarkable happening occurred on the day before I was to leave Lasham. Out of the blue there appeared a Halifax towing what could only be described as a 'prefab' building with wings, but which was, in fact, a Hamilcar glider. The Halifax cast off the glider over the airfield and we all came out to witness this monster coming in to land – and were surprised at how leisurely and smoothly it did accomplished a perfect landing. Later, when I was able to get a closer look at it, I was informed that it could carry a heavy tank, complete with ammunition and crew, but I couldn't help wondering just who would be crazy enough to fly such an aircraft into battle carrying that kind of payload.

Time was to prove that very many brave men would be prepared to do just that.

19.   A Study in Khaki

I arrived at Netheravon to take up my posting to 295 Squadron only to discover that dear old 'R'ecords' had got it wrong once again and that my posting was actually to something called HGMU, which stood for Heavy Glider Maintenance Unit. Mind you, they had only got it partly wrong, because 295 Squadron were indeed at the same station and would be working very closely with us. It was common knowledge that the powers-that-be had decided to create a special airborne force which would make use of both parachutes and gliders. The Glider Pilot Regiment was formed in 1942, and from that moment on, the priority was to get this force operational as soon as possible. The main gliders to be used by British forces were the Horsa and the Hamilcar and these were being produced in very large numbers by many of the furniture making companies such as Harris Lebus and the Norbury Joinery Works. On completion, each glider was given a number and delivered to airfields and various satellite bases in the south of England. We were notified at Netheravon and a record was kept of every glider, for we were now responsible for the maintenance, serviceability and availability of all them.

Because we were dealing with aircraft which were unfamiliar to all of us, repairs to these machines were being carried out on a somewhat hit-and-miss basis, so my first task was to set up a technical library with drawings and maintenance schedules supplied by the manufacturers which could be used when required.

There was of course an intensive training schedule under way, involving both glider troops and paratroops and much of this was taking place from Netheravon. 295 Squadron, equipped with Halifax bombers and a couple of old Whitley and Dakota aircraft provided the carrying and towing aircraft for these exercises. Additional exercises were also being carried out from the other bases where gliders were stationed, the result being that crashed and damaged gliders were spread all over the south of England. All of them had to be retrieved and then repaired, so we were kept fairly busy.

We were at times outnumbered by our khaki-clad friends who may not have been unduly impressed by our standard of discipline but nevertheless respected what we were doing for them. For our part, we realised very quickly what kind of men these were and what a courageous service they were part of. This was made very apparent to me on only the second day after my arrival. 295 Squadron had provided a Whitley aircraft for use by the paratroopers and some 30 or more had boarded for a practise drop. It was about half an hour after take off when the Whitley returned over the airfield and we were all horrified to see that the parachute of one of the paratrooper's had become entangled around the tail wheel of the aircraft and he was being thrown around like a rag doll on the end of a piece of string. We were all wondering what could possibly be done for this poor chap when the Whitley suddenly flew off in a southerly direction and we were informed by another trooper, standing nearby, that he would be taken over Poole harbour, that the aircraft would be flown as low and as slowly as possible whereupon the unfortunate trooper would have to release himself from his entangled chute and hope for the best. This apparently was the drill for an event such as this, but what a decision to have to make. We never did find out exactly what happened to this particular chap, something to do with "closing ranks" I suspect.

And so I began to get settled into my new way of life at Netheravon. I had over 200 carpenter/riggers working in my hangar and we were kept fairly busy due to the amount of flying training being carried out and I was intrigued at the way repairs could be carried out on what I considered to be 'flimsy' gliders.

As regards the Army 'bods' with whom we were working, they were a great bunch of lads: very disciplined and very dedicated, but not very caring about my gliders. The boots they wore could do an awful lot of damage if they were careless where they put them. The majority of their officers were 'Gung Ho' types for whom the whole operation seemed to be one enormous game – 'Well done chaps' and 'Damn bad show' could be heard the whole time. One thing that not one of them lacked, however, was courage, as I witnessed each time a Whitley took off loaded with paratroops or a Horsa was towed off with 40 or more men aboard.

And so service life progressed with much training and many exercises carried out and we all became aware of the urgency of getting these airborne forces to peak readiness as soon as possible.

I had only been on the station for a few weeks when I was told to report to my CO who informed me that I was going on a detachment abroad, that I would be working with 295 Squadron and that I could have five days embarkation leave. That was all he could tell me before wishing me the best of luck.

Rumours, of course, were rife and all four corners of the world were mentioned, but the favourite was that we were bound for the Middle East and an invasion of France from the south ... maybe. With much trepidation I took myself off on my five days leave, although happy to do so as my wife was due to give birth to our first child at any moment. Unfortunately the offspring had his own ideas about arrivals and departures and it was many weeks before I received news of the event, by which time I was lazing under African skies. In the meantime there was much to be done, my replacement was due at any time now and it would be my duty to explain what, why, and how we were doing things because he would never have done anything like this before.

Then, just to make things a little more complicated, it was decided by the airborne chappies that a large exercise would be held almost immediately – using both paratroops and a gliderborne force – which would cover an area embracing nearly the whole of southern England. This turned out to be a bit of a fiasco and we received reports that some of the paras had dropped in for supper or breakfast with various families quite unannounced (some were even offered refreshment). The gliders too had also had their share of mishaps and many had landed off target; those undamaged would be dismantled and reassembled undamaged would be dismantled and reassembled back at Netheravon, the damaged ones would also be returned and would then have to be repaired. As many of the personnel were about to move out this could not have come at a worse time.

After a few days, gliders began to start arriving back and before very long the hangar was full of wrecks, with others being re-erected outside. Although I really would have preferred to have stayed and helped clear up the mess and hated the thought that I was leaving such a lot on someone else's plate, I, and everyone else involved, received our orders to move out and soon we were on our way…

20. Into the Unknown

Returning to Netheravon I found there was much activity and rumour confirmed that our destination was almost certain to be somewhere in the Middle East and that we were to take part in an airborne operation, but it was all very 'hush-hush' and under no circumstances were we to tell anyone about it. We were all issued with khaki drill uniforms, kits were packed and very early one morning we were loaded onto lorries and driven off to Amesbury railway station. The train was packed with airborne forces with all their kit and, as you can well imagine, it was a little congested on the train and many of us had to stand. We found out that our destination was to be Liverpool docks but to get there we went via London and half way round England. We arrived late at night, very tired and weary and were glad to get aboard the ship and get our heads down somewhere.

The ship was the SS *Samaria*, one of Cunard's liners of some 29,000 tons and we were to discover that there were some 4,000 or more troops on board. The ship moved from the dockside at around midnight and anchored well out in Liverpool Bay where it stayed for almost a day. We prayed that no one had mentioned a word of what we were up to, not even to his mum!

By this time we had enjoyed several meals on board and I mean just that. The food was very good and there was plenty of it. Most of the men slept on mattresses arranged in various rooms but officers and senior NCOs were provided with bunks, which made life a little more bearable, although some were not very happy at all. We moved off eventually and sailed out into the Atlantic where we joined up with what appeared to be three more troopships and two destroyers. We proceeded north until we reached the Clyde, where we joined many more ships of all shapes and sizes to form one very large convoy.

Happily, and very gratefully, we also acquired a further six destroyers and a large cruiser, which would be our escorts during our journey. I took a little comfort in the knowledge that someone, somewhere was doing their best to ensure that at least we would arrive safely, even if we might not be coming back...

Within hours we moved off – and what activity! There were ships moving in every direction and although it was daylight Aldis lamps were flashing away and hooters were sounding; it was all a little frightening. I had never seen so many ships together, all moving at the same time and in what appeared to be different directions; most bewildering. But obviously someone was in charge, for suddenly we were all going in the same direction, which was southwesterly. The wind strengthened and the ship started rolling too much for my liking. We were out of sight of land and the effects of motion sickness began to show on the faces and in the actions of many of the lads on deck.

Our first full day at sea was fairly uneventful and we appeared to be making steady progress in a southerly direction. We learned that because we could only proceed at the pace of the slowest vessel in our convoy it would take at least five or more days to reach Gibraltar, which by now we knew to be where we were heading.

On day two at about midday there were two almighty bangs and the ship seemed to shudder from stem to stern. There was no panic but some chaps started counting their beads while others said a few 'Hail Marys' and I got out my lucky rabbit's foot. We were told that it was one of our escort destroyers laying down a couple of depth charges to deter any enemy submarines lurking nearby. Fortunately, this was a one off effort and we had no further bother.

The journey continued uneventfully, which was just as well; had we run into trouble with some 4,500 persons on board I am sure there was nowhere near enough life-saving equipment to go round. Life on board was so uneventful in fact it was very boring. I spent most of my time on deck but it seemed that most of the army lads were involved in card schools below decks. The atmosphere was just awful, as smoking was allowed below, but not on deck. Everyone smoked in those days and the air was very quickly polluted. The situation below deteriorated still further when darkness fell. We were no longer allowed on any of the upper decks, portholes were blacked out and kept shut at all times, there was no air conditioning and what fans that were supposed to be operational were very inefficient and did not help much. This was certainly the worst part of the day for me.

We had been sailing now for several days and the temperature was rising. We were still wearing our service uniform and were all feeling most uncomfortable. We asked if we could change into our KD clothing but were told that this could not be allowed until we had passed the straits of Gibraltar. We were not told why, but at least we now knew for sure where we were heading. We passed the straits at some time around midnight; officers were allowed on deck to witness the event but all other ranks were confined below, which we all thought was a bad show. At least, however, we could now get into more comfortable dress and we all quickly put on our KD. This was to give rise to an amusing incident…

There had come on board at Liverpool when we all embarked, an RAF corporal and an LAC and they had somehow been accommodated among the airmen from 295 Squadron. They were not very sociable and very quickly became disliked because they moaned and complained about everything to such an extent that they were given the nickname 'Jonah and his Wail'. When everyone else put on KD these two, mysteriously, did not … and soon all was revealed. They did not have any. It transpired that they had been posted from Mount Batten to Lossiemouth in Scotland to serve with a squadron of American Catalinas that were to be based there (and you do not really require warm weather clothing up in Scotland). They had apparently changed trains at Salisbury, got onto the wrong train and had finished up in Liverpool. Some bright spark had told them that our ship was going their way and so they hopped aboard. The last I saw of this pair was on the dockside at Algiers, gazing at an American ship which was due to return to San Diego in the States (which was, ironically, where the Catalinas were being built). Perhaps they were hoping to get a lift back to the UK on one of the planes being sent over and if they were indeed successful in achieving this objective then I can only say that this must be the most circuitous route ever taken to get from 'Mount B' to Scotland because the US ship was going home via the Pacific, so they would have almost circled the earth!

On our arrival in Algiers the 'duff gen' merchants started up a rumour that we would be going on to Tunis, which seemed too far away to be feasible. However, we were marched off to the nearby railway station where we boarded a really 'clapped out' old train, the driver, fireman and guard of which were all Arabs; when we were all snugly settled in, the train 'tore' off in an easterly direction at about 15 mph. I do not think we ever exceeded that pace once. We also stopped about every hour, but at least this enabled some of the lads to get off the train and run to the front to get hot water – which the driver somehow extracted from the boiler – with which they were able to make tea. What a resourceful lot! We were on this train for almost ten hours and it was getting quite dark as we approached the Tunisian border. Here we were informed that, due to some political reason, our train would not be allowed to proceed any further and that we would all have to get off.

Our masters, of course, were aware of the situation and lorries were waiting to take us to a nearby tented reception area where we spent the next couple of days just lounging around until a replacement train could be obtained from the Tunis authorities to take us onward.

The postal service, I have to say, under the circumstances, was excellent and wherever we were, letters and cards arrived daily. It was whilst we were at this place (I just cannot recall the name) that I received a photo incorporated in a telegram from my wife (something new that the GPO was doing for servicemen overseas) including a message telling the good news that I was now the father of a fine son. Sadly, my immediate situation did not allow me to celebrate this wonderful event in the way I should have liked, but I did manage to share a few cans of very warm beer with some of my colleagues at the time. Our replacement train eventually arrived and took us on to a place called Kairouan, which was a railhead and so we could go no further. This place was also a 'holy city', which was, I would have thought, the last place to dump our lot. This thought was seemingly shared by the 'higher-ups' because in next to no time we were bundled onto lorries and swiftly taken to our 'home' for the duration of our stay. This place was called Sousse, on the Mediterranean coast and is today one of the most popular holiday resorts in the area.

I was in for a shock, for within a few days of my arrival I was informed that I was to take a party of ground staff to the other side of North Africa to a place called Sale, where there was an American staging post. I looked this place up on a map and found it was near Rabat. Gibraltar was not far away across the straits, which meant I was about to undertake a 1,200-mile journey back to where I had been only a few days before. Dear old 'Records' could not have done better! I was also told that I would not be informed what I would be doing until after I had arrived at Sale...

21. Operation "Ata Allah"

Our attachment to the American base at Sale had all the hallmarks of being both an interesting and rewarding period for us RAF bods. Taking into account the high quality of the meals and accommodation we were offered and the fact that the base was so close to Rabat, all seemed just great and we all hoped that we would be here for a long stay. Rabat was a very pleasant town full of fine shops and stores and wonderful eating and drinking places. There was a very strong French influence throughout the area, the French language was spoken all the time and there was little evidence that the town had been affected by the war in any way – a situation that began to change with the invasion of North Africa by the Allies. The Americans had taken over this part of the area with familiar results: they received top priority for almost everything and prices were going through the roof! Yet everyone appeared to be very happy.

I was very much in favour of the suggestion by the base commander that I should consider a trip to Casablanca and when I put this idea to my lads, most of them were keen too. I made an appointment as soon as possible with the Colonel to discuss the trip in more detail. He asked how many were interested. I told him nine, including me, so he said he would arrange a pass for us all for two days, including accommodation in Casablanca. He had suggested at the beginning that we did this trip by camel (!) and I asked for further details as to how this might be done. He asked me if I knew of the store called JACS in Rabat. When I said that I did, he told me I should go behind this store, where I would see the 'chaps' who would arrange the transport for me. So off I went to find these chaps, expecting to find a bunch of disgraced undergraduates or a crown of disenfranchised stockbrokers trying to make an honest living. Instead I saw this sign above some stables which read 'Camel Hire and Purveyancing Services' (CHAPS) which was staffed and operated by a bunch of Arabs.

There were camels everywhere. I explained my requirements to the 'boss man', Abdullah. He said that there would be no problem, we should all be at the 'garage' by 6.30 am to leave at 7 am as the journey to Casablanca would take 8 hours, due to the fact that we were inexperienced camel riders so we should not attempt galloping! That is some joke! We all arrived well before the deadline, which was just as well, because they were short of a long-distance camel, which would mean a short delay.

At this point I should explain. Hiring a camel in not unlike hiring a motor car; if you need to go far you must make sure you have enough fuel to get you there – so you must fill your camel up before you set our because there are not many filling stations in the desert. The camel vendors were not, however, put out by the particular shortage of one camel as it seemed it was a regular occurrence and they had ways of overcoming the problem as we were about to witness. We had already learnt that only male camels were used for these long distance excursions but no one, up to that point, had told us why. All would soon be revealed!

We were soon introduced to the other members of the staff, Ahmed and Sabu, who were the younger brothers of Abdullah. We were told that Sabu would be accompanying us as our guide. There was a lot of activity in the yard. All the camels had been 'topped up' except for the 'short measure' one, so he was led to a vast water tank where he started to drink. Sabu stood by his head and the other brothers positioned themselves at his rear. The camel kept on drinking solidly, then just when it appeared to Sabu that it had almost finished, he made a signal to his brothers. Ahmed, the taller of the two, lifted up the camels tail as high as he could, exposing the camel's 'goolies'. Meanwhile Abdullah picked up a couple of house bricks and with a nod from Sabu brought the bricks together in a cymbal style fashion around the said 'goolies' with a vigour and fervour that would surely be the envy of a percussionist in any symphony orchestra anywhere! The effect of this operation on the poor camel was, in the first instance, to make his eyes water, something I am sure would have the same effect on you or I in the same circumstances, and in the second instance to make the unfortunate creature take in a very large gulp of water, perhaps the odd gallon or two! "There we are…" said Sabu, "now we have a long-distance camel, so we can go."

After witnessing this extraordinary spectacle I turned to Abdullah and asked "Isn't that very painful?"

"Oh no," he said, with a toothless grin, "as long as you make sure not to trap your thumbs between the bricks!"

Being in close proximity to so many camels I began to
wonder if this whole exercise was such a good idea. These
animals are not the most endearing of God's creatures. One
could love a horse, dog or even a cow but a camel? It is
such a grotesquely-shaped animal, with a disdainful look, a
malevolent disposition and an evil eye. I was beginning to
have grave reservations about the whole trip. However, it
was too late to have second thoughts, we were told to
mount up. The staff had attached a contraption to the
hump of the camel, which to me looked like an upturned
bricklayer's 'hod' made out of bamboo, bits of old carpet
and pieces of leather all held together with string. We were
instructed to climb up on this structure whilst the camel
was in a squatting position, then to position our legs until
they resembled a distorted hairpin! When we were all
settled there was a signal from Sabu and each camel rose to
its full height, scaring the wits out of all of us. I soon discovered why the camel is called the 'ship of the desert' it
pitches, tosses, rolls and wallows and at some time during
its evolution it must have been crossed with a crab because
it moves forwards and sideways at the same time; very
disconcerting for the novice rider.

A short time after we had left Rabat and were entering
the desert proper something made me realise that I had
made a very big mistake. You see, I had elected to ride the
last camel in the convoy, just in case any of the party
should get into difficulties. Now I don't know whether it is
as a result of their diet, or if it is due to all the water slosh-
ing around in their bilges, but camels suffer from severe
flatulence. Well, the camels don't suffer, only any human

who happens to be nearby! To make matters worse, camels are also very territorial and very competitive; they seem to live by the motto 'anything you can do, I can do better', at least, that's what these particular camels appeared to be doing. The prevailing wind in the area was south-east to north-west. Regrettably, that was the direction in which we were going. On second thoughts the camel's competitive nature was perhaps a help to me. The gentle murmur one emitted when 'breaking wind' was greatly magnified when made by many. So when all the camels 'let fly' in unison at least received fair warning and was able to lower my head, hold my breath and, in the words of that old song from the past, 'Wait till the clouds roll by Nellie'!

The journey, apart from being very uncomfortable, was also boring, as we were unable to chat to one another due to our being strung out in single file. After what seemed ages we came to an Arab village where Sabu had obviously decided we should halt for refreshment. At this point a nursery rhyme must have come into Sabu's head, 'Ring a ring a roses' to be precise, for I heard him shout 'Usher, Usher, we all fall down!' And all the camels did just that. It seemed that their legs splayed outwards and then retracted in the manner of a Spitfire's undercarriage. The angle of incidence increased alarmingly (all riggers with their inclinometers fall in) and we were all thrown in the dirt, sorry I mean sand. This exercise, we were informed, was known as 'the dismount', although on this occasion it was not strictly performed in accordance with the Camel Corps Handbook. We picked ourselves up, dusted ourselves down, and followed Sabu to the nearest café, each one of us giving our own impression of John Wayne shuffling off to Boot Hill.

Remounting after the break was again quite something. Most of the lads finished the journey facing backwards. Just as you cannot change your horse in midstream (an old Chinese proverb) neither can you alter your seating arrangement on a camel once you are airborne.

We finally arrived in Casablanca in the late afternoon, all tired, hot, very sore and wondering whether this journey was really necessary. I instructed Sabu to take us to the place where the Colonel had told me to go. It turned out to be a fairly large hotel on the seafront, overlooking the harbour. It had been taken over by American Armed Forces and was used as a kind of headquarters-cum-base which could be used by any Allied forces passing through.

We came to a halt in front of the hotel and went through the 'dismount' ritual again, this time in front of an audience of French civilians and US troops, who naturally applauded this spectacle in a fitting manner. We were allocated rooms where we could sleep and were told that food was available anytime we chose to go to the mess hall. I sent Sabu off with his camels, all ten of them linked to each other, to wherever one would normally take ten camels to park overnight. The first thing I wanted was a bath or shower as I felt so dirty and I was lucky to get a shower straight away. I then felt like a new man who was more than a bit peckish! The Americans had already acquired a reputation for good living and my first meal in the hotel certainly lived up to expectations.

My very short stay in Casablanca was great – but more of that another time. Much more important was something that came about when we all returned to the hotel later that night. In the hotel bar I joined in with some of the American airmen and we got talking about the trip that the lads and I had made on the camels – the terrible journey, sore bums etc and how I was dreading the return trip. A Staff Sergeant among them said that lorries departed for Sale and other US bases every day from the hotel, and asked if he could arrange for us all to go back in one of these lorries would we prefer to go? We had arranged to leave the hotel by 8am when Sabu was to be there with camels in time for us to get 'mounted'. The Staff said that he would let me know the arrangements he had made before then so I went to bed in a very happy frame of mind. Mind you, I did have nightmares thinking of the type of transport that would be required to take ten or more bods and ten camels!

Early next morning the Staff told me that he had arranged for us all to return to Sale on a 3-ton Dodge truck and that we should be leaving at midday. A silly question, I know, but I asked the Staff if we would be taking the camels with us? He replied in Arabic and what he said sounded very rude and I think it meant 'no'! This proved no problem to Sabu when I explained the situation to him who seemed quite happy to go off to find the nearest camel rank, trailing his ten camels behind him. The journey back to Sale took about two hours. For those readers who have no knowledge of Arabic (you should get some in!) the chapter title "Ata Allah" translated means "God's Gift".

If the camel is God's gift then he can keep it!

22. The Leg of the Turkey

On my return from the 'fleshpots' of Casablanca I was informed by the base commander that I could expect the arrival within the next few days of the first Halifax/Horsa combinations which were being sent out from Portreath in Cornwall to us here in Rabat, Morocco. This was a 9½ hour journey over a distance of some 1,600 or more miles, crossing the Bay of Biscay very close to the hostile coast of occupied France and the suspicious coastline of Spain and Portugal. Sure enough, the first glider arrived sometime in the afternoon after an uneventful journey. The Halifax was refuelled by the American ground staff and together with my lads, checks were carried out and the combination was positioned ready for its continued journey across North Africa early the next morning. This was supposed to be the pattern for all further arrivals, but things did not quite work like this for the next visitor...

A combination certainly appeared over the airfield again in the afternoon a day later but this time it was observed that it's undercarriage had been jettisoned and it eventually made a very good landing just off the side of the main runway. They had apparently come under the scrutiny of suspected hostile aircraft and, discretion being the better part of valour, had discarded anything that might delay their progress, having no wish to "hang about". This was all very well, but they did not carry a spare undercarriage assembly and there was no way we could get the thing airborne without one, so now we had a glider lying there like a huge wounded bird, where until we obtained some wheels it would have to stay. I immediately had a signal sent to explain the situation and request a replacement undercarriage; this was to have astonishing repercussions back in England, as I was to learn later. Meanwhile, a spare set of wheels was put aboard one of the gliders being sent to me and we took delivery of these within a few days.

My next problem was to get these wheels fitted on the glider, as we had no jacking equipment with us. The glider was resting on its skid with the port wingtip resting on the ground and the starboard wingtip high in the air – as it was designed to do, to allow the unloading of its cargo during an operation. I was able to get the undercarriage fitted on the starboard side, with some effort on my lads' part, and I then hoped we would be able to raise the port side by getting all my crew and anyone else I could coerce to bodily lift the machine just enough to slip the undercart in place; after all, it was only made of wood! With everyone in place around the wingtip, at my command to "heave" the glider began to adopt a more level attitude until the wheels on the starboard side touched the ground, but then it would go no further and despite renewed efforts by my "hearties" and the sound of what seemed to be many 'Velcro' fastenings being pulled apart there was no further movement, except that which emanated from the bowels of the 'heavers'.

Fortunately, we were helped out by our American allies who brought along a Flying Fortress mainplane jack and whilst I considered this a most ignoble use for such a piece of equipment they were able to do the trick. Incidentally, of the 19 Horsa gliders sent out to me (there were to have been 30; I don't know what happened to the rest), every one of them with this one exception landed with their undercarriage intact so we never used the FF jack again.

We were supposed to take delivery of two gliders a day, but in fact we never received more than one and then not every day, so we had a very 'cushy' time.

Then one day I was informed by the base commander that a shipment of aircraft spares was awaiting my collection at Port Lyautey, just a few miles away. He would be sending me with a truck and driver to collect it the next day. The truck duly arrived, no three-ton Leyland for these Yanks, it was a thirty-ton Dodge and guess what the driver's name was? 'Chuck'. No relation to the other four hundred Chucks on the base, of course.

When we arrived at the dockside I realised why we needed such a truck. There, in all their glory, were *thirty* sets of assembled Horsa undercarriages, complete with parachutes.[2] Yes, this was the result of my message back to England requesting a single set of wheels to get that stricken Horsa airborne. Somebody, somewhere had got the wrong end of the stick.

The undercarts were all loaded onto the truck and taken back to Sale where the chutes were stored in my tent and the wheels stacked on a piece of waste ground nearby,

---

[2] These parachutes were much smaller than the personal pilot's chute and were not made of silk but of very good linen; there were four to a set and

where they would stay, for I just could not see when or how we would ever use any of them. I was later to discover that when my original signal was received in England, working parties were sent out from Netheravon to various satellite airfields where gliders were stripped of their undercarriages – and here they all were!

Several days later I was sitting in my 'office' when one of my lads came to tell me that there was an American GI by the name of Chuck wanting to see me. It was the driver of the truck I had recently had the use of who wanted to discuss with me the possibility of 'acquiring' some of the parachutes we had collected; it seems he had made contact with one of the ladies' dress shops in Rabat and had learnt that, with the war having been going now for over three years some their customers were looking a bit shabby and were looking for dress material, which was in very short supply. I glanced at the mountain of material stacked in the tent, considered that possibly that they would never be required and in the spirit of 'entente cordiale' and to maintain good relations with the female species of our late allies, (at the same time passing a fleeting glance at the fistful of American dollars in the hand of my 'partner' Chuck) I decided to let him have just one of each colour, red, blue, green and yellow, for which he persuaded me to accept forty dollars. Disaster struck the very next day. I decided to go into Rabat to have a good meal and do other things and spend some of my ill-gotten gains, which I did, but on my return I was informed by my corporal, who I had left in

---

they were very brightly coloured and attached to the wheels, legs and struts for when the undercarriage was jettisoned.

charge, that some thieving Arabs had broken into my tent and stolen some of the chutes. He had informed the American security bods on the camp, who in turn, I was later to discover, had notified the local gendarmerie, who were going to call on me later... and this they did, two very officious chaps, one of whom could speak English. I told them that only white parachutes had been stolen (of which there never were any) knowing full well that every Arab wore white or off-white robes and that it would keep them very busy checking that lot for a while. I did notice, however, that they showed a very close interest in my 'stock' and realised that my incursion into the realms of fashion was to be short-lived. I felt it prudent to inform my late partner of events so far, but to locate anyone by the name of Chuck on an American airbase is like looking for the proverbial needle in a haystack; nevertheless I did succeed, whereupon I suggested he apply for a posting elsewhere as soon as possible. Luckily for all concerned (and me in particular) everything settled down and there were no further repercussions.

There is, however, one other event to mention and this was of a disastrous nature. A glider and its towing Halifax, which had arrived the day before, had been refuelled and were positioned on the runway ready for takeoff for their onward journey to Tunisia. All seemed to be in order and at a signal from the American controller the combination moved off and as usual began a circuit of the airfield. Half way round, however, we noticed that the Halifax had released the glider, which was now attempting a landing somewhere way off the airfield. The Halifax, meanwhile, had completed its circuit and was obviously going to attempt a landing. This aircraft had just been completely refuelled, including the huge long-range tanks fitted in the bomb bays – not the ideal occasion to make a landing on what was, literally, scrubland. They were being watched by the whole base. The pilot was obviously having some kind of problem; he was very low and it did not look as if he would make the runway. Sure enough, he undershot and the aircraft crashed heavily just inside the perimeter, exploding into a fireball as it did so. There was obviously no hope for anyone on board, but amazingly the rear gunner was thrown out of the rear turret and survived, unharmed. I and several of my lads were some two hundred metres away from the inferno but could feel the heat even at that distance. The whole area was covered by a thick pall of smoke and I had the greatest of regard for the American fire crews who, draped in asbestos suits, attempted to get to the crew, but without success; alas they all perished.

Two days later I visited the scene. The earth was still very hot and the whole area of the crash site was a thick and solid mass of molten glass with remains of the engines and other parts of the plane firmly embedded within. A sad and sorry episode.

I took delivery of several more gliders, all of which arrived and were dispatched without any further mishap and then one day my liaison officer came over from Gibraltar and told me that we were to pack all our gear and to return to Sousse on the next glider, which would be the last to come out. This news, of course, was not very well received by any of us, for we had all had a great time at Sale. We

each went around the base and said our farewells to the
many friends we had made amongst the American airmen
during out short stay. I went off to say goodbye to the Colonel and to thank him for his help and kindness to us all and
as a parting gift he gave me a box of very good cigars. My
next duty was to go to the main store with my clearance
chit and return the one item I was accountable for, namely
fly strips, together with the thousand or so 'contacts' that
had made it their grave. I was given no rebate on these!
Within two days the glider and tug had arrived from England, had been refuelled and serviced (very thoroughly I
might add, as we were about to travel on this one!) and was
now ready for our journey to Sousse. Toolboxes were put
aboard, together with all our personal belongings and it was
now time for us to embark. This we did with some trepidation, with memories of another recent takeoff still fresh in
our minds.

I had met the two glider pilots earlier; the senior pilot
was 'Jock' and his co-pilot was 'Chalky', two great guys who
told me I could come to the cockpit any time I wanted. Lift
off was quite smooth and uneventful and after reaching a
few hundred feet we started to circle the airfield before
setting a course for Tunisia, at which point, I did go into the
cockpit from where I could see the tug way out in front
with the tow rope connecting both craft. I then looked
down and there was the dispersal we had just left. I could
see our tents and the large pile of undercarriages we were
leaving behind and I wondered just what would happen to
them. A thought did come into my mind and I envisaged
both Arab and French boys hurtling up and down the

'boulevards' of Rabat with a Horsa landing wheel strapped to each leg – after all, we have had scooters, skates, skateboards and roller blades, anything goes. Remember youth has always found some way of getting from A to B without walking, so who knows?

I hope that somebody got some use out of them.

23. Aloft with the Buzzards (Temporarily)

With a last look at Sale behind, the Halifax with its glider in tow headed eastwards for its long haul across the northern coast of Africa to Sousse in Tunisia, some one thousand plus miles away. We were flying at about two thousand feet, the temperature in the glider was quite high and rising and already we were beginning to become aware of what lay in store for us. Turbulence was building, we were experiencing some buffeting and there were ominous noises coming from somewhere with louder bangs now and then, but not yet causing concern. I think we were flying at about two to three thousand feet and I had managed to get my head down like any respectable airman when I was jolted awake by a terrific crash. It seemed we had entered an air pocket and had dropped earthwards for a while until we hit supportive air once more. We had been flying for some two hours or more and it was now approaching midday, the hottest period of the day, which no aircraft really likes, particularly gliders. The next half hour was a nightmare with everyone hanging on to anything substantial. I made my way up to the pilots' area to find out if I should get off. Through the pilot's window I could see the Halifax ahead and the towrope stretching back from it in a straight line. In the next moment the tug had dropped out of sight and we were somewhere above it, still connected by the towrope.

Then, almost immediately, our positions were reversed and the tug was above us. Inside the glider it was mayhem. Fortunately, the spare undercarriage we were carrying was lashed to the floor, but all my lads' toolboxes, together with a large wooden crate, the contents of which was a mystery, were defying the laws of gravity and floating around in space. At that moment I could have told future astronauts a thing or two about weightlessness! We were also to discover very soon what was in the wooden crate when it suddenly crashed heavily onto the deck and burst open – Spanish onions – consumption the CO of the RAF detachment for!

The two aircraft could not withstand all this buffeting while joined together and I was not surprised when the tug released us after the pilot had found what he considered would be a reasonable landing spot and on which our very capable glider pilots did just that; landing with the under-carriage intact so that we could be collected early the next day. After a short recce and a chat with some of the locals who had turned up to see what was afoot, we discovered that we had landed on an old, disused airfield some one hundred miles south of Sidi-bel-Abbes in Algeria and that we had travelled about three hundred miles of our trip.

We spent an uncomfortable night sleeping in the glider, hungry and thirsty, for we only had a few packets of biscuits and chocolates, which we shared around, and to drink we had to settle for some milk that we managed to persuade our Arabic friends to bring us. When it was delivered to us in some kind of not-very-clean-looking skin bag it was drunk with some suspicion.

Sure enough, our tug arrived for us the next morning, though not really as early as I would have wished, and after connecting up our towrope, to the awe and amazement of some hundred or more natives who had arrived from the surrounding districts, we were towed into the air to complete our journey.

We continued as before and flew on for about two hours. The terrain below was very rugged and I realised we were flying over the foothills of the Atlas Mountains. It was also becoming apparent that we were entering turbulence and experiencing some buffeting and in a very short time this had reached serious proportions. At this point the towrope snapped and we had a real problem on our hands. Full marks to our pilot, who sussed out the terrain below, made his decision, jettisoned the undercarriage and landed the glider on very rough and stony ground. Fortunately, the grasses growing there were some six feet tall and wrapped themselves around our skid, helping to slow us to a stop. We were also fortunate in that we had stopped on an even keel; the starboard wing had struck a smallish tree, shearing part of it off, but with the remaining part wedging itself in the branches and keeping us level.

We made our preparations for leaving the glider, at which point we were halted by the senior glider pilot, who informed us that we had landed in what could be 'hostile' territory. He told us that at their briefing before leaving England they had been told that when the German army was in occupation in Libya they, together with their Italian allies, had instilled in the native population an intense hatred of anything British or American. They were told that we would treat them in a very bad way and that we would abuse their womenfolk. In turn the enemy had promised them that when they had won and thrown us out of their country all kinds of goodies would come their way. Apparently all of their propaganda had worked, with the result that the natives were not at all friendly. My memory immediately took me back to my 'goolie chit' days and I hitched up my trouser belt a few notches!

Jock the glider pilot suggested we should check on our 'arms' and see what ammo we had between us. This, of course, was the joke of the century, or would have been if our predicament were not so serious. It was revealed that in our possession we had just one standard .303 rifle, owned by one of the riggers, an individual I had already marked down as a potential candidate for early admission to the Alzheimer's club. When I asked him what ammunition he had, he told me that when he was issued with the gun he had been informed that when the occasion arose for him to use the weapon he only had to ask and it would be given him! To think that he had cared for and carried the thing around with him since the day he joined only confirmed my earlier suspicions.

At least both glider pilots had revolvers and a supply of ammo and it was they who very cautiously opened the ramp door and we all tried to peer out. The tall grasses among which we had landed were well above floor level but suddenly men began to appear from out of this grass, growing in numbers and getting ever closer to the glider. Many of them carried sticks or staves waving them menacingly, striking the side of the aircraft and all the while uttering sounds which we very quickly gathered were not of a welcoming nature. The moment was tense and although our glider pilots tried to talk to them, they did not appear to be in a very conciliatory frame of mind. Then, out of no-where, came our saviour in the form of an Arab member of this hostile mob speaking some words of English. He told us he worked at a nearby American airbase and produced a signed pass to say he was on leave. He also told us, very reassuringly, that his mates gathered around were not really hostile, just very concerned that there would be no fire risk with our aircraft among the dry grass and that they would like us to take our plane somewhere else.

With the help of our newly found ally we hoped to get some idea of where we were, although, we were sure that our tug would have reported our whereabouts and that we would be contacted in some way before too long. We asked our friend 'Moses' (we had decided to name him so, for after all, he had come down from the mountain and we were hoping he was going to lead us to the promised land) what sort of menu was on offer at the local restaurant. He looked us over and, I thought, me in particular, as though he was looking for a sacrifice, at which point I though of possibly a chicken or two that we could cook ourselves. Unfortunately his English had not progressed that far and I was reduced to sign language. I must have made the wrong sign along the way because in a very short space of time we were inundated with baskets of eggs that I hoped had origi-nated from chickens although I feared some had not. How fresh they were we were to find out later.

From our friend I discovered that we had landed near a village called Khenchela, some two hundred miles from the Tunisian border. We were resting quite high up on a plateau amongst a lot of rocks and boulders, with the front of the glider only about fifty feet from the edge of a gully with water flowing some twelve feet at the bottom of it. It was obvious that we had been extremely lucky to have landed safely; only a glider could have done so, and full marks to the pilot for such a skilful landing. There was no way this glider would ever get airborne from here. We learned from our friend that there were only small villages about and that the nearest large town, called Tebessa, was about 150 miles away and it was here that the Americans had an airstrip and where he worked. Sensibly, we decided to keep to the vicinity of the glider, taking the advice of 'Moses', who said we could have trouble with some other villagers. We decided to sit tight and wait for further developments.

The biggest problem facing us all was what we were to do for food and drink. We did a quick stock take among everyone and turned up a fair assortment of chocolate, some biscuits, a few small cakes and a surprising quantity of soluble coffee in small bags. We also had a very large case of Spanish onions, so things could have been worse. Our friend offered to get us a couple of metal cans in which we could boil up water, but only if we promised to light any fires at the bottom of the gully, near where the water flowed. This we gladly agreed to and were able to boil eggs and some of the onions and have a hot meal. Because there was very little to do it was not long before we were all thinking of bed and although we had learned from 'Moses' that there were no wild animals in the area, there were feral cats and snakes about and so it was decided that we would all bed down in the glider, where a very hot, smelly and uncomfortable night was not enjoyed by all. As you can imagine the next day was a drag; we had exhausted most topics of conversation among ourselves, we could not explore too far, it was terrifically hot and the interior of the glider was like an oven. We mostly read what little was available beneath the shade of our mainplane and prayed we would be rescued soon.

My concern was mostly to do with how we were living and the food we had to eat. The previous day we had eaten only one meal of 'E&O' (eggs and onions) and the air within the glider that night left much to be desired! Today we would be eating at least three or more of these same meals with the odd bar of chocolate thrown in for good measure and the future prospect was daunting, to say the least! It was apparent that the combination of eggs and onions, when passed through the human digestive system, resulted in a gaseous by-product and I envisaged enough of this being generated within our glider to get a barrage balloon aloft. I felt it prudent to put up a notice saying 'no smoking or naked lights please'.

We did not get airborne that night and after eggs for breakfast and approaching E&O for lunch, out of the blue, an RAF officer and an American serviceman turned up to collect us. By way of thanks to our Arab hosts we gave them the glider, complete with its handbook and followed our saviours some 300 yards down the side of the mountain until we reached a roadway and a waiting truck. This took us on a five-hour journey to the American airbase, where an RAF Albemarle aircraft was waiting to take us on to Sousse.

We were asked if we would care for a meal before we took off and you can well imagine what the response was. It was, I have to say, one of the best meals I have eaten and with the added benefit of no by-product!

On a 'lighter' note [and please forgive the pun] I have thought a lot about that diet we lived on for a few days and with petrol soon to reach £5.00 per gallon perhaps someone wise or enterprising among you can put E&O together and provide us with fuel for the future...

24. Tunisia 'n' Trauma (TNT)

The reason for the explosive title to this chapter will be revealed as you read on... The flight back to Sousse aboard the Albemarle was a new experience for me. As there were so many of us, space was at a premium and I was lucky enough to get the place usually occupied by the bomb aimer. Normally on take off the bomb aimer would be seated, but due to the present situation I was required to take up my position, lying face-down in the nose of the aircraft, which was made completely of clear Perspex and afforded a wonderful downward view. Our take off was smooth but my downward-facing position so close to the ground gave the impression of moving so fast that I felt rather uncomfortable and was relieved when the ground started recede as we became airborne. All too soon our journey was over and we were preparing to land and once again I began to get that feeling of apprehension as we began to lose height and the ground came ever closer – but the brakes worked and we finally stopped – home at last.

So now we were back to our tented compound and having to 'rough it' again after the luxury we had experienced over the past few weeks. Everyone seemed so busy and there were quite a lot of glider exercises going on, with resultant damage that kept my lads out of mischief. I spent much of my time going around to other airfields from which many of the Waco gliders were to operate, and of which there were quite a few, trying to scrounge any spare bits and pieces that I required. We still had not been informed of the actual date of the invasion, although we were aware that it was to be Sicily, but we knew that the day of the lift off was now very close and that was why there was so much activity. At times I felt I had wandered into an unrehearsed fire drill in a lunatic asylum.

It was into this 'tranquil' setting that one Major Peniakoff decided to pay us a visit. The gentleman in question was better known, particularly to the German Africa Corps, as 'Popski'. The Major had heard that we were in the area and of the sort of 'capers' we were up to and wondered whether his army could adopt anything we were doing for their own purposes. However, after a very short time spent looking around and talking to one or two people he decided that Horsas and Wacos and what was involved in their delivery were not for him.

The PPA (Popski's Private Army) were specialists in aircraft sabotage and had been a thorn in the side of the enemy throughout the whole of the desert campaign. Their favourite weapon was a cigar-shaped incendiary device which they inserted in the fuel tanks of German aircraft when they were parked on the ground and well behind enemy lines. They had been a continual embarrassment to the German army for years, being a motley bunch, drawn from many nationalities and owing no allegiance to anyone except Popski. They were dressed in a variety of khaki clothing without any badges of rank whatsoever. They were all aware of their prowess in the field and I was told that during a conversation with some of our officers, including the CO, a wager was made by Popski that his men could infiltrate our airfield on any one of three nights and sabotage the powered aircraft on the ground by marking each aircraft attacked with the sign 'PPA'. Despite intensifying the guard on our aircraft, the day after the second of the three nominated nights some 80% of our aircraft carried the tell-tale letters PPA! The following day a retaliatory raid was carried out on Popski's immaculate tented encampment and a variety of typical 'service rubbish' was deposited on the camp from a low-flying Albemarle. PPA honour was at stake, they had been caught napping and there was much consultation resulting in a visit to our base where a few enquiries were made. Among Popski's band of brothers was a Welshman by the name of – you'll never guess – Wilfred, and because we almost spoke the same language we kind of palled-up and it was he who came to my tent and asked me the question that he had been sent to ask. The question was 'when is peak shitting time and when do most of you go?' I replied it was between 7.00 and 7.30 am and he would not say another word. I later discovered that this same question had been asked in other quarters and I very soon had my suspicions about what might be in store. That night, saboteurs secretly invaded our camp, removed the latrine covers and inserted weak, suitably timed detonators into the 'ordure', replaced the tops and then withdrew. At the appropriate time, vantage points were unobtrusively occupied by the PPA.

Success! So many shirt tails, so many bare bottoms and so much 'ordure' were never seen before or since! A truce was successfully negotiated.

Popski and his men bade us goodbye and he said he would look us up again when we got to Syracuse (he obviously knew more that we did) and things returned once more to normal.

We then heard a rumour that the day of the operation was to be July 9th – now only just over a week away. The invasion area around Sousse comprised several airstrips from which tug/glider combinations would lift off, a few tented sites that provided accommodation for many of the glider pilots and air-landing brigade, and storage huts and tents for the storage of arms. Explosives and ammunition were located in nearby olive groves, away from the camps, and all had been erected by the Americans before we arrived. The main base from where the Horsas would take off was where the RAF contingent was billeted.

It was the afternoon of July 6th, only a few days before what had now been confirmed as the 9th for take off, when there was an almighty explosion. I was in our Nissen hut at the time and I rushed out to see what had happened. Many of the airborne forces were at the time actively engaged in cleaning their weapons and checking over their arms and explosives and for a moment I thought some clown had withdrawn the pin from a primed hand-grenade and dropped it. More explosions followed and they were even more violent. I looked up to see if we were being attacked from the air and then there was another enormous eruption; the ground below me was shaken and from a distance of about half a mile a huge column of black smoke was rising from where I knew the olive groves were. I was then informed that an ammunition dump had caught fire and that a thousand tons of explosives had been blown sky high. What was worse was the fact that the whole dump hadn't gone up at the same time – parts of it were still exploding and were showering mortar bombs and phosphorous grenades all over the landscape. Unfortunately we happened to be downwind of this eruption and so were showered with bits and pieces. I think it was feared at one moment that this upheaval would jeopardise the imminent operation and it might have to be postponed, but due to the resourceful British and the magnanimous Americans, somehow and somewhere replacement supplies were found and, as there had been no loss of life, everyone was happy.

Final preparations went ahead, there was now very little air activity and not a lot for us to do. The American ground crews were to be responsible for the assembly and marshalling of the tugs and gliders ready for lift off. American Waco gliders, which would be mostly towed by Dakota aircraft, would make up most of the invading force. Some, however, would be towed by Albemarle aircraft and these machines did their task admirably. Only seven Halifax tugs were available for towing the Horsas but the other was towed by an Albemarle – and quite successfully.

When the day for the operational take off eventually arrived the glider pilots and the air landing brigade had been on our base for the past two days, cleaning their weapons and checking over their arms and it was a little disconcerting to see so many grenades and mortar shells lying around.

The time for take off was to be at 18.30hrs. The tugs and gliders were all in position, had all been connected and were positioned in a double herringbone pattern down the length of the strip. Final inspections were carried out, all heavy loads were lashed down securely and all that remained was for the human cargo to arrive, and this they did right on time. You would have thought that these men were going on holiday, they were so jubilant, laughing and joking – and not into a battle from which too many of them would not return. Brave men indeed!

The American ground crews were to be responsible for sending the air fleet off and so my lads and I were to be spectators. "Load up, get aboard," came the order and in a few moments every man was in his appointed place and a kind of quiet descended on the strip. Suddenly, as though from nowhere, the sound of a lone piper was heard and seen marching along the length of the strip in front of the gliders playing 'Flowers of the Forest' – a fitting send off for these men for sure.

It was now time for take off and in response to a signal the idling motors of the tugs roared into life and the first machines started to roll. After the first take off the airfield was completely shrouded in a blanket of dust and sand swept up by the tugs' propellers and after the first few had gone it was impossible to see anything; from then on everyone was flying blind. The fact that all combinations became airborne safely says much for the skill of the aircrew.

Finally they were all off and the air became clearer and we watched the last formations disappear into the distance as they headed towards Sicily…

25.   Sicily Disaster

Our gliders all having taken off safely, the airfield now returned to its solitary state, leaving a feeling of anti-climax. We retired to wherever we chose to go, each with our own thoughts on what was in store for the men we had just sent off. The whole operation, codenamed 'Husky', called for three further lift-offs within the next couple of days, supplying both gliderborne troops and paratroops, but no further take-offs were made from our strip and I don't think any more of our Horsas were used.

Within 24 hours of our first assault on Sicily by airborne forces, news began to filter through that it had been a terrible disaster and a new phrase was introduced into the English language, courtesy of our American cousins – 'friendly fire' (the old name for it was 'an almighty cock-up'!). The news we were getting from Sicily was that a thousand or more of our airborne troops, both English and American, had been killed. It appeared that many of the American tug pilots took a dim view of the anti-aircraft fire being put up as they approached Sicily and just dumped their gliders in the sea, some up to five miles from the coast, where most of the soldiers drowned. Furthermore, many tug/glider combinations had been shot out of the air by the invasion fleet and their naval escorts who had mistaken them for enemy aircraft and opened fire, with devastating effect.

This operation was the first major Allied airborne assault made on enemy territory and was mainly planned and carried out by the American command, with a token effort supplied by the British. It was therefore the American's responsibility to ensure that the plan was sound and that everything went according to plan.

It is not my desire or intention to comment on the outcome of events relating to this debacle, this has been done in many subsequent books and by more qualified persons than I. I would, however, like to mention one book by Geoffrey Regan, the *Guinness Book of Flying Blunders*, in which he writes and I quote:

> "Airborne troops have always been among the elite in modern armies. They are often called upon to risk their lives before even encountering an enemy, leaping out of a plane and falling, perhaps in pitch darkness, swinging helplessly below their chutes at the mercy of the enemy firing at them from below, or in the case of gliders just sitting in their seats helpless as their glider slowly picks its place to land. Such men deserve at least the assurance that should death find them early it will at least not have been at the hands of their own comrades, the Sicily fiasco, however, deprived thousands of these elite soldiers of even this comfort, their numbers were laid waste by their own colleagues, their own pilots and those of their allies, the most disgraceful example of all amicides. Their murderers – for no other word adequately describes what happened during this airborne operation – were legion and you will not find anywhere an official report of this operation. There is one I am sure but it will be buried somewhere deep in America for when General Eisenhower received the final report from General Patton the facts were so disgraceful he de-

cided that the whole fiasco must be hushed up. There were just too many reputations at stake."

There were many rumours going around as to what was now to happen. Despite what had happened to the airborne assault, the invasion as a whole had been successful. We were told that our forces were advancing and that we would soon be going on to Sicily. I was then informed that I should present myself to the transport section the following day, complete with all my worldly goods, for transport to Tunis. There was no further information supplied as to what this was all about, but I thought 'Sicily here I come...'

Next morning I discovered I would be travelling by road aboard a Chevy truck, together with five glider pilots, a sergeant, three staff sergeants and one commissioned officer, a first lieutenant. None of these had any knowledge of what our trip was about; that's what they told me anyway. The driver of our transport was an American GI whose name, of course, was Chuck and I assume he had driven at least once before but not a Chevy, as we were soon to discover.

I sat in the front with the driver and we set off, very quickly reaching Mach 1 – or so it appeared to me. Our driver went so fast, slowed for nothing or nobody and was slumped over the steering wheel at such a peculiar angle that for a while I thought he had suffered a heart attack. I asked the lieutenant to give him a prod just to make sure he was alive. As we approached one of the smaller villages along the way, still going like a bat out of hell, we crossed a zebra crossing and knocked down what I thought were a couple of penguins. I am almost certain that that is what they were, but if they weren't, the local nunnery was going to be two nuns short for vespers that evening. When I pointed out to Chuck what I thought he had done, he said he was asleep and had not seen anything!

We pressed on regardless and at this breakneck speed we were going to reach Tunis well before lunchtime. This was something to look forward to, as none of us had had much breakfast and we must surely be stopping there. But no. We did reach Tunis in a short while, but like the proverbial 'dose of salts' we went through it like lightning and kept on going. We travelled on for almost another hour, when either Chuck's foot slipped off the accelerator or his boot-laces became entangled around the brake pedal, because we stopped outside what had once been a very upmarket hotel.

Our acting commander in chief (i.e. Chuck) told us to go inside, saying that this was where we would be staying and where we would be informed of our next move. We discovered we were at a place called Bizerte, a seaport some 30 miles north of Tunis. We were informed that a ship would soon be arriving and that it would be taking us home. I, of course, was dumfounded, but my army colleagues knew of this all the time, but had not let on.

Before the war, Bizerte had been a secluded holiday resort, a favourite place for wealthy Italian, French and Egyptian nationals, who kept their yachts in the harbour nearby. The hotel in which we were to stay had been taken over by the Americans in line with the invasion plans relating to Sicily and was used mainly for emergency purposes, but they could also provide some food. We six new

arrivals decided that as we were going home we would pool
all our foreign monies and have a really decent meal at a
restaurant nearby, which had been highly recommended.

There was certainly a discrepancy when it came to pool-
ing the money. Guess who had most – me – and who had
none – the officer. I was not too surprised, as during our
journey I had gathered that the army were not all that well
paid and these airborne lads in particular; apart from their
basic pay, parachutists received two shillings a day extra but
glider pilots only one shilling, because parachuting was
considered the more dangerous. After Sicily, I thought this
ought to be reconsidered.

After freshening up we went for a walk around the town
before dinner and enjoyed a cold beer, of sorts – something
we hadn't had for some while. I decided that I would start
with 'soup of the day' but nobody was forthcoming as to
what it was. When it arrived there was a cockroach lying at
the bottom. I complained the waiter, who told me meat was
on ration but as he had an affinity with the RAF he had
given me their ration for the week. I fished it out and sent it
waddling back to the kitchen from whence it had come.

For my main meal I ordered the speciality of the house
which was to be 'Goat's Scrotum en Croute', which could
possibly have been very good, but I was rather put off by the
very local Arabs who kept coming into the restaurant and
enquiring as to the whereabouts of their pet dogs and cats
that had suddenly gone missing. But the wine was not too
bad. There was no red – I think the waiter said it was all
being used for 'transfusions' (it was, after all, the same
colour and the end result was much better). For the first

time I witnessed white wine being decanted from an American jerry can. It wasn't bad, but considering how much of the stuff we drank and where it came from we did not get much of a 'lift'.

The next day we were informed that we would be staying for at least three more days, by which time a ship would arrive to pick us up; this duly arrived and was none other than the Cunard liner *Franconia*, a vessel of some 25,000 or more tons. It had anchored some way offshore, for Bizerte had no facilities for such a huge ship. We were to be transferred to the ship by a 'lighter' from an American destroyer which was moored just outside of the harbour.

We were completely surprised by all this. Surely this monster vessel had not called here just to pick us up, even though we considered ourselves very important people? Come the transfer time, we were taken out to the ship and as we approached I became aware of just how large and tall it really was. A ladder had been lowered from its upper deck, not a rope ladder but real steps, which somehow were fastened to the side of the ship. From our little boat, bobbing in the water, they appeared to extend up to eternity.

We had to climb up these steps (thankfully it was daylight) a frightening experience I do not want to repeat. Within a short time of boarding I was aware of movement and yes, we were on our way to 'Blighty'. We learned that some very high-ranking persons had come aboard at the same time as ourselves, so we really were not the main reason for this unusual stop. I did wonder, however, just what was ahead for me. Perhaps I would be going to rejoin the RAF…

26. All at Sea

Here I was aboard the SS *Franconia*, sailing westwards towards Gibraltar and, unbelievably, going home. It was still warm, the sea was calm and very blue and everything was so very pleasant. There did not seem to be many people aboard, many more ship's crew than passengers. I had been given a cabin to myself, although there were bunks for four others. The main meal of the day was between twelve and two and unfortunately I had missed it, but tea/supper was between half past four and six and this I did not miss – and how splendid it was.

After a very comfortable night's sleep I awoke to find we were anchored just outside a very large port, which I was soon to discover was Algiers. Immediately after a very fine breakfast the ship began to move and in a short while we were tied to the dockside, where we observers witnessed a very interesting exercise. A gang plank was positioned from dock to ship both fore and aft and then, marching across the dockside and walking up the gangplanks were none other than the very same RAF personnel we had left behind in Sousse and who had come out to North Africa aboard the *Samaria*.

Once everyone was on board we set sail again and headed for Gibraltar and out into the Atlantic, all wondering what was to happen next. Uppermost in all our minds was, of course, whether there were any submarines about.

We had no escort, but our ship had a very good turn of speed and we would rely on this. Our journey proved uneventful and also very pleasant and I think gave us all time to reflect on whether our sojourn in Africa had really been necessary. From an RAF point of view it had achieved little and cost an awful lot. The Americans, who were responsible for the airborne side of the Sicily invasion, could quite easily have mishandled things without our help. Most of us, I think, were of the opinion that there would not be another such airborne operation; this one had been such a debacle. After all, the Germans, who were the pioneers of this form of warfare, never again attempted to use massed airborne forces after their heavy losses at Crete.

All good things have to end and, after a very pleasant five days on board this magnificent liner, we found ourselves again very near to home. Everyone, it seemed, was feeling elated. None of us, I am sure, had thought we would be home so soon. We were all of the opinion that we were to follow the advancing army through Sicily then Italy and then through Europe. Happily we were wrong.

We were not sure at which port we would be docking. The home port of the *Franconia* was Liverpool, but as the first sightings of Old England came into view a cheer went up from everyone on board and a feeling of euphoria was experienced by all. We were met on the dockside by, I believe, men from Records or 'Movements. I was sent off on a few days leave and told to report back to Netheravon, much to my disappointment.

On arriving back at Netheravon it did appear at first that nothing had changed. The powers-that-be had obviously decided to proceed with the use of these glider things in spite of their shortcomings. The theory was that if you put 40 soldiers in one glider they would all be together when they landed (unless the glider was blown to pieces before it landed) whereas if you threw 40 soldiers out of an aircraft on parachutes they would be scattered somewhat. This was open to debate, I must say, but meanwhile we carried on as before. I did discover that whilst I had been away we had added to our stockpile of gliders considerably and now had almost two thousand of various types scattered over the south of England. With the decision to persevere with airborne operations there were many exercises called for; the airborne forces were being enlarged and there was a very intense training programme under way.

I have mentioned in previous chapters that I consider the airborne forces were indeed a great body of men, well disciplined, brave to the point of recklessness and highly intelligent. They were mainly led by officers with a 'gung-ho' mentality, but nevertheless just as courageous. It was not hard, therefore, to be sure to get total support for any difficult or dangerous project that might be on offer. The reason I have included this reminder is that, since my return to Netheravon, I had been made aware of a few of the more crazy antics those airborne Johnnys got up to when your back was turned...

One of these was known as 'the snatch racket' and involved the positioning of a glider ready for take-off some place on an airfield whereupon the appointed tug aircraft would fly towards it and attempt to 'snatch' it off the ground and into the air. These experiments had been going on for some while. For a time they were carried out at the testing site at the RAE Farnborough, but I think the boffins there had become alarmed at some of the harebrained antics of the airborne lads and had asked them to take their gliders elsewhere. So they transferred their activities to Netheravon.

The whole idea behind the snatch scheme revolved around a winch that would be attached to the floor of the towing aircraft. Its reel of cable would be fed through the rear and attached to this would be a hook which, it was hoped, would engage with the towrope of the glider. This in turn had been formed into a hoop and suspended between two posts some distance from the front of the glider. When the towing aircraft had successfully 'hooked on', the winch cable would start to unreel and a built-in clutch would engage and apply increasing tension to the connecting reel, thus softening the 'jerk' on the towrope and allowing the glider to be pulled into the air without being pulled to pieces. It might sound like an impossible feat, but it worked. However, to say it was 'a bit hairy' would be an understatement. It was not achieved without cost to both army and air force aircrew.

The first combination this was tried on was a Whitely/Hotspur that was not entirely a success but after this progress was made we finally managed to get a Horsa aloft towed by a Dakota. The reasoning behind this snatch programme was to enable the retrieval of undamaged gliders from a battle area in which they had landed and so we were never required to snatch fully-loaded gliders, something I am sure we could not have done. The snatch programme was taken even further when the SOE considered using it as a means to pick up their agents who were returning from occupied territory. It was decided that tests would be carried out and someone had the bright idea that one of the sheep that roamed around the area could be used for this purpose and would be attached to the towrope and placed beneath the loop above it. An Avro Anson was used on this occasion and all would have been well had the sheep not panicked and bolted when it heard the noise of the approaching tug... Assorted lamb dishes were served in the mess for the next few days!

The snatch was then tried using a dummy and then eventually a man (same thing, this one in uniform). When I saw him sitting under the loop, looking towards the approaching tug, I wondered just what would be on the mess menu for the next few days, but it was a success and he soared aloft like a puppet on a string. I do not think this idea was ever used by the SOE but the Post Office showed interest and I learned that this operation was carried out on their behalf during the Falklands war.

Another crazy experiment involved the use of 'restrictive parachutes'. The whole idea of using gliders was to get men and materials into strategic areas as quickly as possible without the enemy being aware. To do this the glider should land as fast as possible after release and braking parachutes were considered. I witnessed one such experiment with a Horsa glider. The Dakota towed it over the airfield and released it at about 300 feet; the pilot put the glider into a dive, increasing speed and at about 50 feet the parachute started to open. The glider appeared to hang in space for a few minutes and then just fell to earth, hitting the ground with great force and raising a cloud of dust. The wings both fell off, the undercarriage went up through the glider floor and every one on board got off several inches shorter than they were when they got on...

One more idiotic idea was known as the 'Bayes Carrier Wing' – in effect a pair of wings joined together by a slender tube in which the pilot would squeeze and which would be attached to a tank. It had no conventional undercarriage, but a trolley that would separate from the tank on take off. This also applied to the wings, which would also be discarded. A half-scale model was made of this thing and many tests were done with it, but when some glider pilots were asked if they would fly the real thing it proved beyond the limit of insanity. They all said 'no' for, in addition to piloting the glider, once they were down they would then become tank drivers. The idea was shelved.

One of the craziest ideas of all was to attempt to snatch a fully-loaded Hamilcar glider, complete with its huge cargo of a tank, ammunition and crew – a feat the boffins at Farnborough said just couldn't be done. Two ideas were considered, one was to attach rockets at the wing tips. I never saw this used and I think the idea was dropped, but I did witness the second option... this was referred to as the 'twin-tug tow', which meant that two Halifaxes and a Hamilcar glider would be sitting on the runway with a rope from tug to tug with a quick release incorporated and looped through a pulley, attached to the Hamilcar. This was to be a formation take-off with the Hamilcar in the middle at about 1000 feet. The formatting tug throttled back slowly, the rope slipped through the pulley until the quick release operated and released the formatting tug, allowing the leading tug to tow the glider to its destination. It worked, but only because the aircrews of the two Halifaxes were well above average. As far as I know this operation was never repeated and the idea was dropped.

All of this scatterbrained experimenting, of course, kept the workshops busy and provided some interest in what otherwise would have been a very boring existence. The Day of Atonement was nearing and we had to put more into getting ready for the invasion and so happily the nutcases were put to one side and we could almost have a normal life at last.

27. Beginning of the End

The following few months were indeed very busy ones for the airborne forces, but for me and my airmen working in our workshop it was much as before. You will have gathered by now that I had become very despondent with my attachment to this whole undertaking. I no longer seemed to be part of the RAF; everything related to the Army and this part of it in particular. I know the RAF got it wrong sometimes, but this lot excelled at making blunders and I was very unhappy about it all. The Commanding Officer of the airborne forces at that time was General Browning, known to everyone as 'Boy'. The RAF liaison officer between the airborne forces and us RAF personnel was a Wing Commander White, who had also acted in this capacity during our venture in Sousse. These two stalwarts had got together and decided that, for the duration, the airborne forces would be known as 'Boy's Boys' and us as 'Chalky's Chicks' and you will understand why I felt a little fed up with being a part of what was a very serious business.

To understand a little more just how I felt, I was made aware that 'D'-Day must be getting near when, within the space of a week I received three separate deliveries of large wooden crates. Two of these contained hand torches, twenty thousand of them and another crate held the batteries for them – three per torch! Three more crates contained – wait for it – Thermos Flasks! When I enquired what these had been sent to me for I was told they would be fitted in each glider but that no decision had been made yet as to whether the operation would be at night or if the flight would be of some duration. They were never fitted but everyone on the station soon had a torch and a Thermos flask. The remaining crate held our secret weapon. This was a silhouette shape of a Horsa glider cut out of thin plywood. There were three different sizes, the wingspans being one three and four feet. The mainplanes were pinned at the root and folder back over the fuselage. There was an elastic band fastened at each wing tip and again fixed to the nose of the fuselage, which also had a piece of lead attached to it. These were then packed in bundles of ten and held together by a strap with a quick release fastener, operated by a length of string. The whole idea was to take these aloft in a plane and release them a short distance from the real dropping zone. The release would operate, the elastic would come into its own and in the searchlight glare these silhouettes would, it was hoped, draw off the anti aircraft fire. You can fool some of the people... etc. These were also never used, as far as I know.

I was to receive yet another surprise delivery when a truck driver turned up in my office one day. "Are you HGMU?" he asked, and when I confirmed that this was so he told me he had two hundred and fifty gallon cans of striped paint for me. I looked at the calendar on the wall thinking it was maybe April fool's day but it was actually June 1st. Thinking that I should humour this one, I asked "What colour?" and he replied, without the trace of a smile "black and white". At this point I thought I should pass this one over to my boss in the adjoining office and when I told him about this chap and his 'striped' paint he too asked, "what colour?" I knew then that I had *two* nutters on my plate! Within a few seconds, my boss was in my office. He told me to get just a few of my lads to help and to get this paint unloaded as quickly as possible and out of sight and to get the whole lot covered so that it could not be seen by anyone. 'All very secretive,' I thought, and seeing the look on my face he told me that I would learn shortly what the paint would be used for. Two days later I found out...

With effect from reveille on the third of June a complete blackout was imposed on Netheravon as it was on all service bases all over the south of the country. This involved no-one entering or leaving a station; only with a very special pass was this allowed; even married personnel who lived off camp were not exempt. Phones could not be used either we were completely isolated. This of course had to mean the invasion was about to start and the 'powers that be' wanted to keep it a secret. These 'powers' had also learned some lessons from the Sicily fiasco and here is where the 'striped' paint made its entry, to ensure that on the actual operation our participating aircraft would not have to worry about 'friendly fire'. It was decided that all allied aircraft – both gliders and powered – taking part in the operation would be identified by black and white stripes painted above and below the mainplane surfaces and other designated areas. For the next two days it seemed that everyone on the station was in possession of a paintbrush and I was reminded of some advice which was given me when I first joined the RAF. It was that if I was ever in doubt two things were paramount: 'if it moves, salute it and if it is stationary, paint it'.

Having finished our paint job the authorities were notified and the invasion was put in motion from early morning on the 6th. The surrounding airspace was filled with aircraft and gliders heading for the coast of France and what lay ahead. As I had experienced in Sousse, a sense of anti-climax was apparent and I think everyone was just waiting for any news that could be told by the tugs when they returned. It was to be three days later when I was told to report to Wing Commander White's office, where he told me, in the presence of three other senior NCOs, that an airstrip had been laid just off the beach in Normandy and that we would be flying out to France the next day. Our mission, we were told, was to carry out an examination of all the gliders that had landed on the three dropping zones at the time of the actual invasion with a view to assessing any damage sustained in the landing.

This was joke number one ... and joke number two was for us to decide whether, in our opinion, any of these gliders could be flown back to England. Somebody, surely, got a medal for thinking that one up! We eventually flew out from Netheravon aboard a Dakota aircraft, not the next day but the next night at about nine o'clock. This was either to prevent the enemy knowing we were coming or perhaps because someone was feeling a little uncomfortable around the buttocks! The first half-hour or so was quite uneventful and then someone began to welcome us with a display of fireworks that we could see out of the portholes as we approached the coast of France. I must admit I was enjoying this display of many different coloured lights coming towards us until one of the aircrew told us "it is friendly fire" and I too experienced a little tightening of the buttocks. But we survived, made a very good landing, taxied a very short distance and disembarked into what appeared to be chaos.

There were figures rushing about and shouting, lots of noise around and it was all taking place in pitch darkness with only the occasional glimmer here and there. I do not think I have ever experienced such darkness since. We four NCOs bedded down in a tent for that one night, but don't ask me how we got there. In the morning we found we were in a small field that housed several mobile vehicles being used for communications, map printing, etc and also where General Montgomery resided during this initial stage of the invasion. We actually saw him as he went off to work that morning and he waved as he went by. Just down the road there was a tremendous battle going on and yet he seemed so matter of fact.

Our CO, Chalky White, had somehow acquired a jeep and we four NCOs piled on board and were taken off to our appointed site to carry out our specified duty. The sergeant I had with me had come from the glider salvage section at Netheravon and was a chap I knew. When we were put down at the DZ which we were allocated to cover and saw what was before us we just gulped. We were looking at a very large field, overgrown with grass some four to six feet tall, from which protruded tall iron posts which had been embedded in the ground in a haphazard manner to form an obstruction to anything trying to land … and it was in this field that our gliders had put down. The Horsa glider had a large, hinged door on its port side which, when lowered, provided a ramp down which its cargo – a Jeep and a six-pounder gun – could be unloaded. This could only be used, however, if the glider had been landed on its skid and allowed to rest with its port wing tip resting on the ground. The tail section of the glider was also fitted with quick release bolts to allow for a rapid exit, but this method was not much in favour with the troops. We soon noted that the glider troops under operational conditions had resorted to a much more practical method of exiting the glider. Although somewhat unorthodox, it did achieve positive results, and this was to toss a hand grenade deep down into the tail section of the glider. (This method, I must add, was frowned upon).

It was into this field of crashed and damaged gliders that my sergeant Bill and I gazed. We clambered over a five-barred gate and started to carry out our inspection of what appeared to be all unrepairable wrecks. The weather was fine and warm, there was much activity going on all around and lots of explosions in the distance. We had been working for about an hour and I suppose we were happy to be by the seaside and enjoying the sea air with no one to bother us when suddenly, from out of nowhere, a very guttural voice ordered, "You two, put your hands up. Don't move an inch and keep perfectly still." (As if it was possible to do one without the other!) Fright set in; I could hear a sound coming from my sergeant's direction not unlike the sound a coffee percolator makes when it has finished its task and from the vicinity of my knees came the distinctive sound of 'bongo drums' being played! Then, out from the long grass popped a little man dressed in a camouflage jacket and the green beret of a marine commando who said, in what I now realised was a broad Scottish tongue, "Allo, allo, what's going on 'ere then?" He had a 'Tommy gun' that he kept pointing at me and I had to give him a reasonable answer to his question. My mind went back several years before I joined the RAF when I was confronted with a similar situation and I had to provide an answer.

At the time a company known as 'The Times Furniture Company' employed me and they had sold a new double bed to a young married lady and she complained that when traffic passed by her bedroom window the bed vibrated and made noises. They had sent me to investigate and after lying on the bed whilst traffic flowed I could find nothing wrong and told her so. "You wait until a double-decker bus goes by," she said, so back on the bed I went. In fact we both lay on the bed, waiting patiently. Now it chanced that her husband had decided to leave his office early that day and, of course, he walked into the bedroom and was a little shocked. "Hello, Hello... What's going on here?" he asked.

"You are not going to believe this but I am waiting for a bus!" I replied.

Our 'Jock', however, proved to be more amenable and accepted my explanation without question. He told us that we were lucky to be alive for the uniform that we were wearing, having become soiled by all the dust that was flying about, looked very much, from a distance, like German 'field grey'. He normally fired first and made enquiries afterwards. He suggested that if we chose to pursue our idiotic mission we should get into khaki clothing; and that we certainly should not do any further inspections in this field as there were enemy snipers in the surrounding hedges. He thought that the only reason we had not been shot at as we walked around was because we looked like German troops. Taking all this advice very much to heart, my sergeant and I dropped like stones to the ground and, giving the most realistic impersonation of a pair of lizards, made our way to the five-bar gate. In negotiating that obstacle I am sure I would have been the envy of every limbo dancer from the Caribbean.

We made our way back towards the coast towards where we were billeted. We knew that it was somewhere near a place called Ranville and as we got nearer to the shore we came to what had once been a café of sorts, badly damaged and around which there were a lot of soldiers milling, some drinking mugs of tea and munching 'wads'. Feeling a little 'peckish' we wandered in to see what was on offer and who should be there than none other than our 'Chalky' with several 'brown types'. He wanted to know what we were doing there and when I told him what had happened and what our Scottish Commando had said about our 'dress for the day' his comment was, "How dare the man! If we are to die, we shall die in our own uniform!" This, I thought, coming from the security of way behind the action, just about 'took the biscuit'.

Following these events it was decided that possibly the whole retrieving exercise was a little premature and that we should return to base. But this was easier said than done, as no aircraft were available. All returning aircraft were needed to transport wounded personnel back to Blighty and there was no shortage of these. The temporary harbour being constructed at Arromanches was as yet unfinished but was being used for special reasons. As I was a very special reason I was told that if I could find a ship to take me I could go that way, which indeed I did, and eventually landed back at Netheravon...

28. Closing the Hangar Doors

Back at Netheravon again, little had changed. It was much quieter, although there was still some activity from the 'airborne Johnnys' – the odd glider or two would take off on some clandestine mission, but for myself it was a very quiet period. This situation was the pattern to be for the duration of the war, my lads in the hangar kept reasonably busy with odd repairs, not to mention a respectable output of wooden toys for the nearby hostelry for children. I was not involved in any way with the other two major glider operations, namely the Arnhem fiasco (Operation Market-Garden) and the Rhine crossing (Operation Varsity) and when it was finally all over I was a very happy man for other reasons than the general one. I could now hope to get back into the RAF once more, for I was convinced that glider warfare was on its way out, as indeed it has proved to be.

The immediate aftermath of the war brought a few problems with the release of so many men all due for demob. We at Netheravon had large numbers of aircrew sent to us whist their demobilising documents were prepared and, as we were already short of clerical staff, a backlog built up and there were many frayed tempers. I suddenly discovered that I was the senior NCO on the station and all these disgruntled airmen were my responsibility. I needed to find outlets for them to vent their spleen. The biggest problem was to stop them 'going over the wall'. The station CO

decided that it would be a good idea to hold a full colour
hoisting parade every morning, together with accompanying inspection, and I would have the responsibility of
arranging it, just as a station Warrant Officer would do. Of
course, the whole thing was a shambles; most of these
aircrew had been lucky to escape with their lives and were
in no mood to play soldiers. Most of them did, however,
turn up on parade, but their uniform left much to be desired, their buckles, badges and buttons having a not
unattractive 'greeny glow' about them. The words 'metal'
and 'polish' had disappeared from their vocabulary some six
years earlier and their standard of drill left much to be
desired. Discretion, again proving the better part of valour,
our CO adjusted his decision of holding parades daily to
weekly, much to the joy of everyone concerned.

Out of this charade came a benefit to yours truly. The
Commanding Officer called me to his office to tell me that
as I was carrying out the duties of station Warrant Officer I
should be given that rank and that he would put the wheels
in motion to achieve that end. In the space of a few weeks,
sure enough, there appeared on SROs notification to the
effect that I had been promoted to the dizzy heights of
'acting Warrant Officer' with pay, with effect from '18-6-
1846'. That's right, 1846! In the spirit of the occasion
(wasn't everyone feeling elated) I decided to write to the
Paymaster pointing out that according to SRO dated at that
time, I felt I was due a considerable amount of money in
backpay and allowances.

You can imagine my surprise when I received a letter
back from the Air Ministry, acknowledging my claim and

informing me that I was indeed entitled to, in their estimation, the sum of fifteen thousand pounds! Their letter went on to inform me, however, that it appeared I had overlooked a paragraph in King's Regulations under which a Commanding Officer is personally responsible for any losses accountable.

If the CO is killed, or had not been appointed, the responsibility devolves upon the next senior officer or non-commissioned officer; in this case it appears to be you. We have before us invoices as follows:

20,000 Hand Torches @ 6s each	£6,000.00.00
20,000 Thermos Flasks @ 7/6 each	£7,500.00.00
Decoy Gliders	£ 249.00.00
250 Gallons Paint @ £5.0.0	£1250.00.00
2 Pks American Flystrips	£13.08
Total	£14,999.13.08

As all these items are now accountable, the responsibility for this sum of money now falls upon you. We are, therefore, crediting your account with the sum of three shillings and four pence, this being the difference between the two amounts. We are sure you will find this in order.

My elevated position was not to last very long. I had previously applied to go on a jet engine course at No 4 S of TT at RAF Locking and my posting came through just two weeks after my 'promotion'. Of course I had to revert back to my old rank and was never adorned with the coveted 'Tate and Lyle' symbol.

For some time before I left Netheravon I had been having feelings of sickness and occasional pains in my chest. The service doctor told me that I was suffering from dyspepsia and that I should stop drinking tea but these symptoms continued after I arrived at Locking and steadily became worse until I eventually had to go in to hospital in Bristol. There, it was diagnosed that I had a peptic ulcer. An operation was not really necessary at that stage and they would try to disperse the ulcer with drugs. This would mean my staying in hospital at Locking for several weeks to see what happened. On presenting myself at the sick bay for admission, I asked one of the inmates who was passing by "what's it like in here?" to which he replied "the food is bloody awful and they give you so much it makes me sick sometimes!" I wondered if I had wandered into the nut house by mistake!

My stay in Locking sick quarters was quite pleasant, my medication was very simple and I had very little discomfort. In fact I felt much better than I had felt for quite a while. You can imagine how I received the news that I would have to be discharged from the service on health grounds and did I have any objections? It was now December 1946, Christmas was a week away and I was told I might go home for the holiday, as I was now much better. I was given a diet sheet but was still taking my pills and on my return in the New Year a final decision would be made about my continuing to serve in the RAF.

During my stay at home over the holiday I was able to discuss my future with my wife and other relations and came to the decision to stay in the service if I was given the choice. Returning from leave in January I went back to sick quarters to complete my treatment and within a couple of weeks I was visited by a Group Captain of the medical branch who had come to discuss my future. He was very open and honest, telling me that as the service was, at this particular moment in time, very short of experienced staff he felt he could 'pull a few strings', as he put it, and could perhaps keep me in. He told me, however, that there were a few things to consider, one being that I could not expect any special treatment regarding diet or any consideration about where I may be posted, also, that in his opinion, without care and attention to diet and mode of life, although I was now cured of ulcers they could well return within the next five years. If they did return in five years I would then be much nearer to a pension consideration and he was sure that, should they return, nobody would be able to keep me in the service long enough to draw a pension. I was given a week to decide.

I had enjoyed my life in the RAF and the service had afforded me many benefits. I had met and made friends with a very wide spectrum of people, there had always been a very wide choice of sports in which to participate and I had become involved in many aspects, to my utter enjoyment. This was all fully encouraged by the service chiefs. Apart from the 'bull' and an occasional duty the main 'gripe' was the lack of money we were rewarded with at the end of the day. Thank heaven for the clothing allowance and weren't we careful with our uniform?

I have to say that I always felt very proud to be in the RAF. I still do today; my period of service was a great moment in my life and one that I have never regretted. That I had to leave was sad but I did have a young wife and a very small son and I felt my real duty was to be with them, so I had to say farewell and bid the RAF goodbye. I was to be sent to a place called Squire's Gate that was the demobilising base for RAF personnel and it was here that we were issued with our 'demob' clothing. I think this airfield had been used pre war as a civilian airfield but at this point in time it had just two small hangars. The only reason I am mentioning this is that I was being transported on a dear old Leyland truck to catch a train at Preston to travel to London, when we had to stop at some traffic lights and looking across at the airfield on my left two chaps were closing the hangar doors, very appropriate, I thought. "Bye Blokes!" I called out to them, as they performed a duty I had carried out in the past and would no longer be doing. I began to realise just how different my life would be from now on, for surely there can be no comparison between service and civilian lifestyles. Yes, I was feeling very sad to be leaving the RAF; after all, I had spent the best part of fifteen years of my life in the service, throughout my youth and into manhood, which also took in the war years. I seemed to have had a very eventful life.

I can't recall how long it took my train to travel from Preston to 'the Smoke'. I do know, however, that by the time I arrived I was in a much better frame of mind. The future prospect of sharing a full life with my new son and my wife, with whom I had spent such a little time so far, made me feel much better and made me decide that, yes, from this day on the hangar doors would stay SHUT.

That's all lads… I hope you enjoyed my memories and that they gave you the occasional laugh.

~ END ~